AF469303

A FIRST COMPUTER DICTIONARY

A FIRST COMPUTER DICTIONARY

Brian Samways and
Tony Byrne-Jones

Devised by Lionel Bender

First published in 1984 by
Macmillan Children's Books
a division of Macmillan Publishers Limited
4 Little Essex Street, London WC2R 3LF and Basingstoke.
Associated companies throughout the world

Created, edited and designed by Lionel Bender,
10 Chelmsford Square, London NW10 3AR,
in association with Madeleine Bender.

Authors	Brian Samways
	Tony Byrne-Jones
Educational adviser	Martin L. Jackson
Text editor	Mike March
Art editor	Patrick Nugent
Illustrators	Hayward and Martin
	Radius
Typesetting	Facet Filmsetting

British Library Cataloguing in Publication Data
Samways, Brian
A first computer dictionary.
1. Microcomputers–Dictionaries,
Juvenile
I. Title II. Byrne-Jones, Tony
001.64'.04'0321 QA76.15

ISBN 0-333-38378-8
ISBN 333-38379-6 (paperback)

Printed in Hong Kong

Introduction

This dictionary is written for beginners of all ages, and in particular for people using a home computer. The common technical terms, abbreviations and jargon words of computing are defined and explained.

The book covers all aspects of computing from its history and development to the uses of computers in everyday life. It clarifies how computers work, the various parts of a computer system and the language used when writing programs.

The dictionary entries are listed in alphabetical order. Each consists of a definition written in clear and simple language. Many entries are accompanied by an illustration, table or chart to give greater understanding of the subject. Within definitions, some computer words you may not know are printed in **bold** type to show that they are explained, under the appropriate letter, in the book.

Abacus

An early counting frame, made of beads sliding on wires, used for arithmetical calculations. It is similar to a modern computer in that multiplication and division are done by repeatedly adding or subtracting.

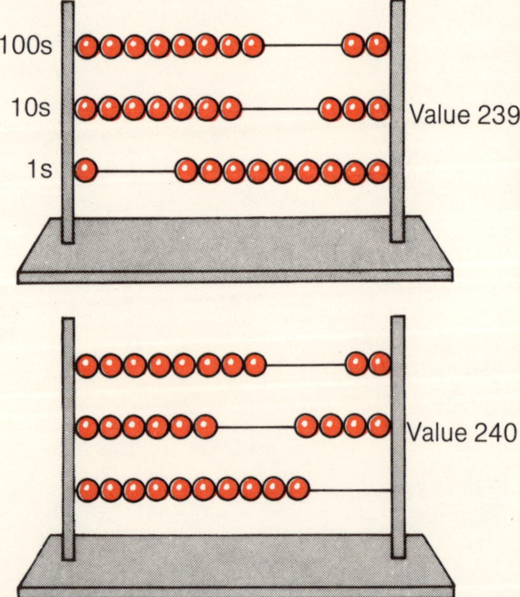

Abort

To stop the running of a **program**, usually when it is not proceeding in the expected or required manner. Control is then returned to the **operating system** of the computer.

Access time

The time the computer takes to carry out an instruction to get stored **data** and have it ready for use. If the data is stored in the computer's main **memory**, the access time will be shorter than if it is stored on **cassette tape** or **disk**.

Accumulator

A special place, or **location**, in the computer's arithmetic and logic unit (**ALU**) used to store the latest answer when doing calculations. The location is known to the **operating system**, and so may be accessed directly and quickly.

Acoustic coupler

Acoustic means to do with sound: the coupler allows **binary code** to be sent from one computer to another, via a telephone line, using only two sounds, one for 0 and the other for 1. In this way any **data** can be transmitted over long distances quickly and economically. See also **modem**.

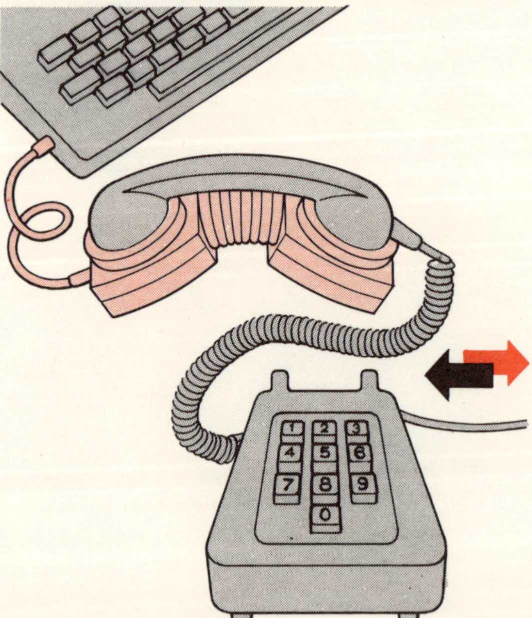

Acronym

A word made up from a descriptive phrase, usually by taking the first letter or letters of each word in the phrase. Although they are sometimes unclear to newcomers, acronyms are regarded as useful 'verbal shorthand' by regular users. Common examples include: **ASCII, BASIC** and **RAM**.

Adder

An arrangement of **logic gate**s inside a computer used for adding together numbers. Calculations may require either a **half adder** or a **full adder**.

Add-on

Any extra piece of equipment that can be added to a computer system. Those that are added outside the computer are also known as **peripheral**s.

Address

A precise place or **location** within the computer's memory where **data** may be stored, and later accessed. Each address is numbered, so the data can easily be found when it is needed. This keeps **access time** to a minimum.

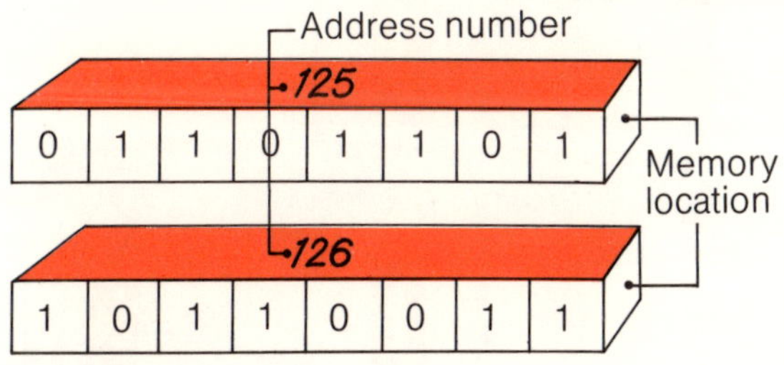

Address bus

Inside a computer, the sets of wires, or route, along which signals travel to each **address**. **Data** to or from an address then travels via the **data bus**.

Adventure game

A computer game in which the player or players take part in some adventure, solving problems and taking decisions which affect what happens next. Use of a **graphical display**, together wih colour and sound, can make the games very exciting. Many of them offer a competitive challenge by allowing the skill of the players to be measured and compared.

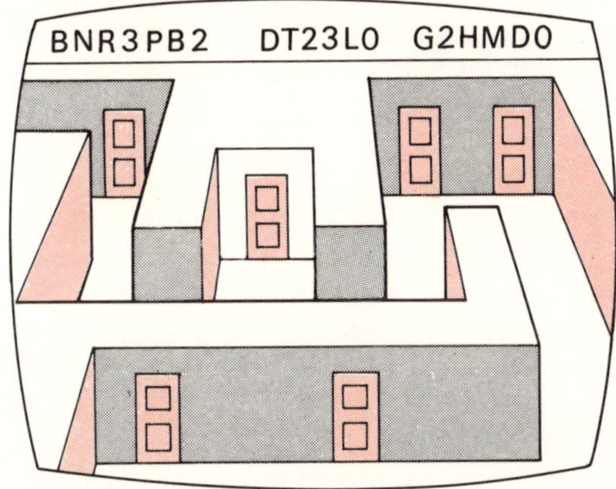

Aiken

Howard Aiken (1900–73), an American scientist, first proposed the idea of the ASCC (Automatic Sequence Controlled Calculator). This electro-mechanical machine, the first ever automatic **computer**, was built in the mid-1940s. The program instructions were supplied using **paper tape**.

ALGOL

ALGOrithmic **L**anguage. A **high level language**, developed in Europe, very useful for solving mathematical and scientific problems.

Algorithm

The detailed steps that need to be taken to solve a particular problem. These first have to be thought out before they can be put into a computer **program**. The results of different starting values can then be found knowing that the same steps have always been followed. See also **flowchart**.

Alphanumeric keyboard
An **input** device that has keys for both the letters of the alphabet and numbers, and usually includes other characters found on a typewriter, such as punctuation marks.

ALU/Arithmetic and Logic Unit
The part of the **central processing unit** where calculations and **logic** operations are done. It includes a pigeon hole, or **register**, for holding the results of calculations during processing.

Ampersand
The sign '&'. Normally used in place of the word 'and', but also accepted as computer jargon to mean 'the number that follows is in **hexadecimal notation**', i.e. it is not a number in the usual tens (**decimal**) system.

Analog(ue)
A word used to describe something that changes continuously rather than by jumps, e.g. temperature, voltage, speed, rotation. Readings of such measurements can be fed as **data** into computers, using a suitable **A to D converter**.

Analogue computer
A machine that works on **analogue** values, accepting the measurements as they occur, and from one or many sources. Such computers are said to operate in **real time**, and can therefore be used to monitor and control other things, or events, as they are happening. At the same time information can be **output** in the form of tables, etc. to enable visual records to be kept, or as magnetically stored data for future use.

Analytical engine
A mechanical calculator, designed by Charles **Babbage** around 1833, which depended upon a complicated set of gears in order to function. Engineers of that time could not make the machine to the high degree of accuracy required, and it thus gave uncertain results from its calculations.

AND gate
One of the **logic gates** used within a computer to control the flow of **data**. An AND gate will seem to output a pulse only if all its inputs have pulses. It is used to find the carry **digit** when two binary digits are added. To chart the results for two or more inputs, a **truth table** can be constructed using 0 to indicate 'no pulse' and 1 for a 'pulse'.

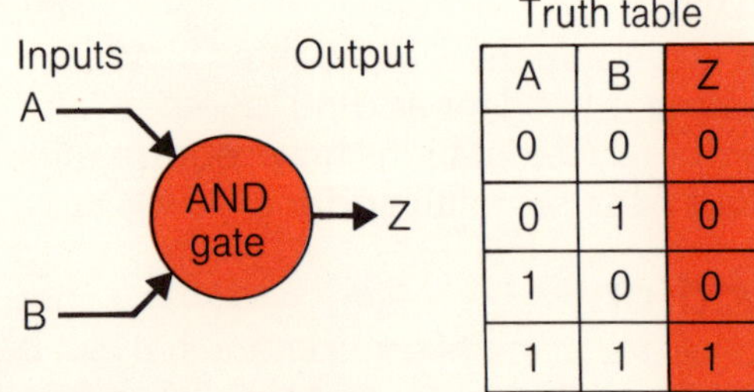

A	B	Z
0	0	0
0	1	0
1	0	0
1	1	1

Animated graphics
Moving characters, or charts, parts of diagrams, graphs or games pictures displayed on a computer screen that changes as fresh data or instructions are keyed in by the user or input by the program.

Applications package

A set of **programs** written to do a special job or series of jobs, together with the necessary written instructions and description. The jobs might be anything from producing charts and tables relating rainfall, wind and temperature, for weather-forecasting purposes, to calculating a company's finances.

Archived file

A file that is not in current use, but is stored away from the computer, on **disk**, **cassette tape** or other **media**.

Arithmetic and logic unit

See **ALU**.

Array

An ordered way of storing **data** in a computer's memory so that it can be accessed by its position. See **one-dimensional array** and **two-dimensional array**.

Artificial intelligence

'Learning' from what happened last time; a **machine** that uses a **program** that improves itself each time it is **run**.

ASCII code

American **S**tandard **C**ode for **I**nformation **I**nterchange. Each **character** is given a numerical value, so that data is easily understood when transferred between parts of a computer system. The coding can also assist in sorting data into numerical and/or alphabetical order.

Character	Binary code	Decimal equivalent
SPACE	00100000	32
!	00100001	33
"	00100010	34
£	00100011	35
$	00100100	36
%	00100101	37
&	00100110	38

Character	Binary code	Decimal
'	00100111	39
(	00101000	40
)	00101001	41
*	00101010	42
+	00101011	43
,	00101100	44
—	00101101	45
.	00101110	46
/	00101111	47
0	00110000	48
1	00110001	49
2	00110010	50
3	00110011	51
4	00110100	52
5	00110101	53
6	00110110	54
7	00110111	55
8	00111000	56
9	00111001	57
:	00111010	58
;	00111011	59
<	00111100	60
=	00111101	61
>	00111110	62
?	00111111	63
@	01000000	64
A	01000001	65
B	01000010	66
C	01000011	67
D	01000100	68
E	01000101	69
F	01000110	70
G	01000111	71
H	01001000	72
I	01001001	73
J	01001010	74
K	01001011	75
L	01001100	76
M	01001101	77
N	01001110	78
O	01001111	79
P	01010000	80
Q	01010001	81
R	01010010	82
S	01010011	83
T	01010100	84
U	01010101	85
V	01010110	86
W	01010111	87
X	01011000	88
Y	01011001	89
Z	01011010	90
[	01011011	91
\	01011100	92
]	01011101	93
^	01011110	94
_	01011111	95
`	01100000	96
a	01100001	97
b	01100010	98
c	01100011	99
d	01100100	100
e	01100101	101
f	01100110	102

Assembler
A special program in the computer that changes an **assembly language** program into **machine code**.

Assembly language
A **low level language** using abbreviated instructions that can easily be remembered by the user e.g. JMP means 'Jump' and LDA is the abbreviation for 'Load **accumulator**'. An assembly-language program first has to be converted to **machine code** by an **assembler** before the computer can carry it out.

Assignment statement
The instruction to give a certain value to a **variable**. Thus, LET A=40, or just A=40, assigns the value 40 to the variable A.

Asynchronous
To start the next task as soon as the present one is completed, without needing to wait for the next **clock** cycle.

Atlas
A famous **second generation computer**, one of the first to use **transistors** instead of **valves**.

A to D converter
Electronic device that changes **analogue** signals to **digital** by testing them at very short intervals and giving them a value that can only increase or decrease in regular steps.

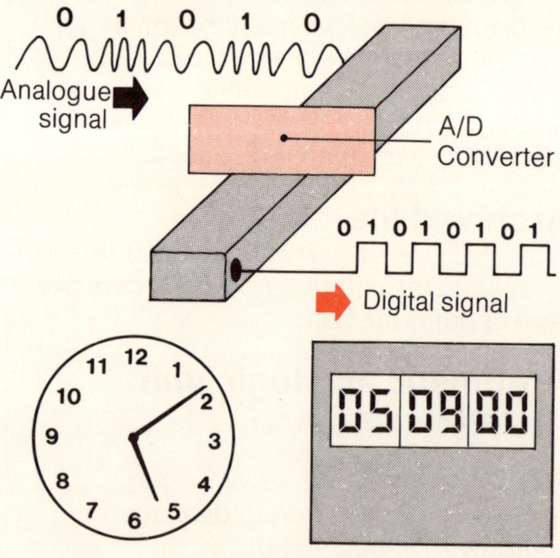

Author language
A program allowing someone with little computer experience to make 'learning packages' that will be of use to people studying a particular subject.

Auto-start
The ability of some computers to **load** and **run** a program automatically. Thus they are ready for use as soon as they are switched on.

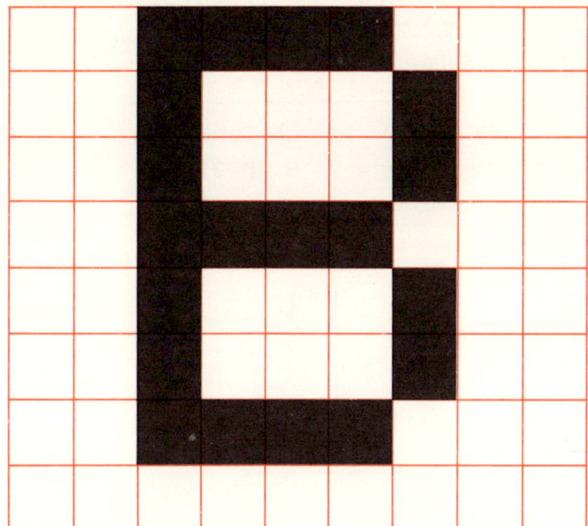

Babbage
Sir Charles Babbage (1791–1871), an English inventor and mathematician, often called the 'father of computing'. His Difference Engine, a system of gears like those on a bicycle, was designed to do sums and produce tables of figures by calculating the differences between groups of numbers. Basically a giant mechanical calculator, it was left uncompleted in 1833 after 12 years' work. He went on to design the **analytical engine**.

Background
The colour of the computer screen whether on a television set or VDU. **Graphics** or text can be printed on it in **foreground** colours.

Backing store
A **store** for data that is not needed immediately by the computer. It usually consists of **cassette tape** or **disk**. The data can easily be loaded into the main memory when required.

Back-up
Duplicate copy or copies of **data** already recorded. This is a safety measure in case, for instance, the original is wiped clean or recorded over by mistake.

Bar code
A pattern, or code, made up of printed black lines, or bars, of different thickness. The pattern is usually read by a **light pen**, and the data fed into a computer. Commonly used in shops and warehouses for instant pricing and stock control, and in libraries for recording out/in details.

BASIC
Beginners' **A**ll-purpose **S**ymbolic **I**nstruction **C**ode. A **high level language** designed for educational use which is easy to learn and simple to use. **Program** lines are numbered, and the computer follows the instructions in sequence. A simple BASIC program to add any two numbers, A and B, and display the result, C, could be

```
10 INPUT A
20 INPUT B
30 C=A+B
40 PRINT C
50 END
```

Batch processing
A system whereby the computer is not used until all the programs and data needed are gathered together as a single set or batch, so that only one **load** and **run** instruction is required.

Baud rate
The rate at which **bit**s are transmitted, measured in bits per second. Commonly 300 and 1200 bits per second (baud) when loading a **microcomputer** from cassette tape. Can be as much as 1000 million baud for the flow of data along an optical fibre cable. Named after a French telegraphic pioneer, Baudot.

Benchmark
A task, or series of tasks, performed on different computers to compare their speed, accuracy and efficiency.

Bi-directional printing
A printing method in which the print head moves across the paper and back, printing in both directions. Thus, the first line is printed left to right, the next, right to left and so on. Common on **dot matrix printer**s.

Binary code
A code made up of two digits, 0 and 1, which the computer uses to store and generally handle all kinds of data. 'Binary' comes from the Latin 'bi-' meaning two. The 0s and 1s of the code are called binary digits (**bits**, for short). They represent the electrical pulses flowing through a computer – 0 is a nil or low voltage and 1 a higher voltage. These can be thought of as either of two states – the 'off' and 'on' positions of a switch or the 'up' or 'down' of a railway signal.

Binary notation is a number system in which all numbers are made up from 0s and 1s (the binary digits). This is in contrast to, say, denary notation – the decimal system of everyday use. Here numbers are made up from ten digits, 0 to 9.

In binary notation, the highest digit that can exist in any column is 1. So, when adding binary numbers, 1+1 equals 0 carry 1, or 10. Thus a binary 1 doubles its value each time it moves one column to the left. (A binary 0, of course, is just a 0 wherever it occurs.) Binary numbers are therefore written in columns of ones, twos, fours, eights and so on.

Binary	Decimal equivalent
Column values	
8 4 2 1	
0 0 0 1	1
0 0 1 0	2
0 0 1 1	3 (2+1)
0 1 0 0	4
0 1 0 1	5 (4+1)

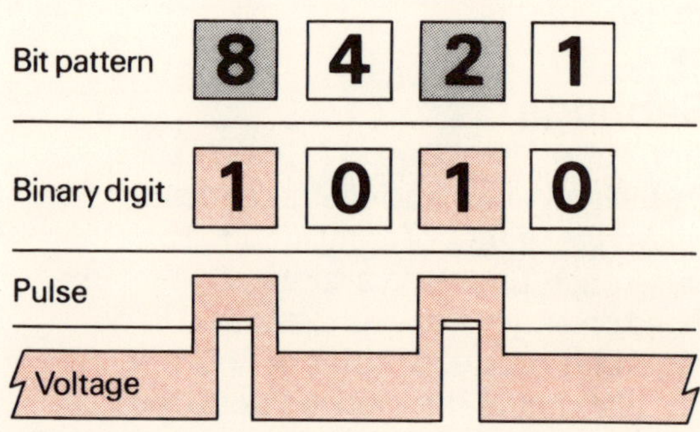

Binary fractions
A binary number made up of two groups of **bits** separated by a point, in which that part of the number to the right of the point is a fraction. Like binary whole numbers binary fractions follow the rules of binary notation. See **binary code**.

Here is an example of how to convert a binary fraction to a decimal fraction: 101.101 in binary becomes 5.625 in decimal.

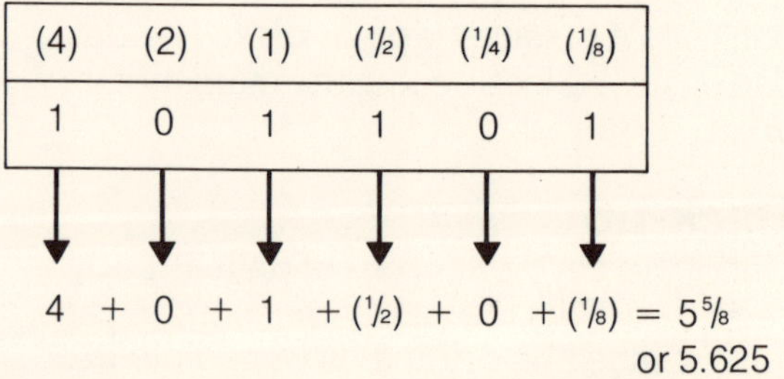

Bit
Short for **bi**nary digi**t**. There are two binary digits ('bi' means two), which make up the **binary code**. They are 0 and 1. A bit is the smallest unit that can be stored in a computer's memory.

Bit pad
See **graphics tablet**.

Black box
Any part of an electronic system that the user knows what it does and how it relates to other parts in the system without having to understand how it works. Examples include an **AND gate**, a binary counter and an amplifier.

Block diagram
A simple diagram consisting of labelled boxes joined by arrowed lines, showing the flow from one part of the system to the other parts, e.g. what happens between typing a letter at the **keyboard** and its appearance on the **screen**.

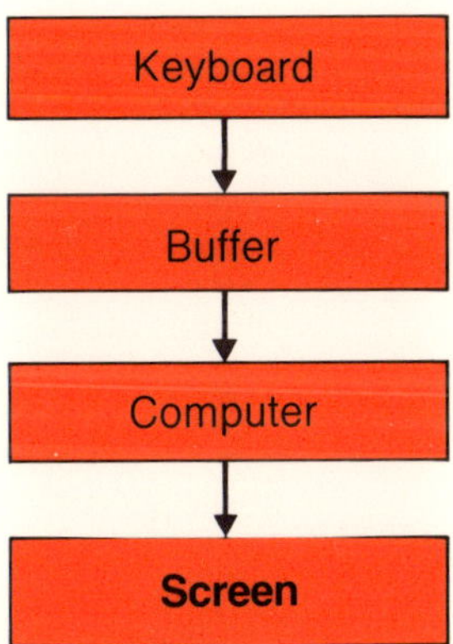

Boolean algebra
A set of rules, written by the Irish mathematician George Boole in 1847, that allow logical statements to be tested using yes/no, or true/false responses. Used with computers because this true/false method suits the binary (1 or 0) way of working. The results of such tests are presented in **truth table**s.

Booting
Unless using **auto-start** a computer, when it is first switched on, awaits instructions from the user before running a program. By pressing a certain key, or keys, routines will be followed that will prepare the machine for use. This process is known as booting or bootstrapping.

bps
Bits per second, essentially a measure of the **baud rate**.

Branch
A programming instruction telling the computer to stop at that point and jump to another part of the program. The instruction can be unconditional, when it will always be carried out; or it can be conditional, when the decision depends upon a value. For example, if the answer is YES, go to line 80 in the program, if it is NO, go to line 70.

Breadboard
A circuit board made up by hand to test the working of assembled components. Used by manufacturers to design and construct electronic circuits.

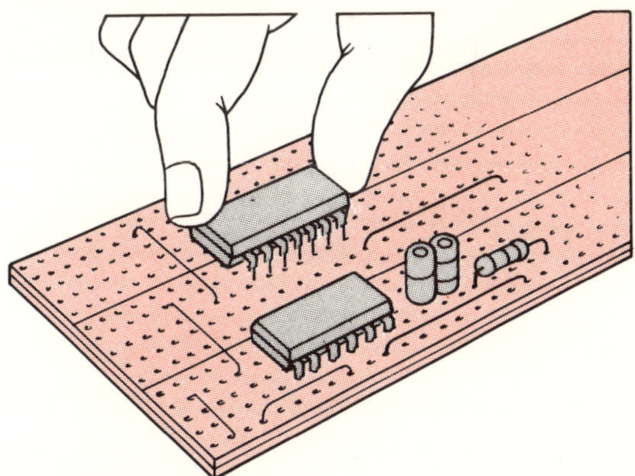

BREAK key
The use of this key will always stop the computer and will often erase most of the contents of its temporary memory. On some computers, called **stop** key.

Bubble memory
A means of storing **data** using magnetized bubbles on a chip. The bubbles are magnetically moved across the chip to a reading head, which records the presence of a bubble as 1 and its absence as 0. Bubble memories are tiny, with no mechanical parts, making them ideal for storing large amounts of data. The data is not lost when the computer is switched off.

Bubble sort
Nothing to do with bubble memories, but a program for sorting data into an orderly form, e.g. from the most expensive to the least expensive. Starting at the top of the list, the computer compares each piece of data with the next, and moves it up the list as appropriate (rising like a bubble). This process is repeated over and over again until all the data has 'bubbled' into its right place.

Buffer
A temporary memory store for data that is being moved to or from a computer or a **peripheral**. Often needed because of differences in their working speeds.

Bug
An error in a **program** (may simply be a typing error) or the **operating system**, or a fault in equipment. Very often stays hidden for some time, before showing itself with unpleasant results, hence the name.

Bus
See **address bus** and **data bus**.

Byte
A set of **bit**s, usually enough to represent one **character**, that is handled by the computer as a unit. Most **microcomputers** have eight-bit byte systems, and so a byte generally means eight bits.

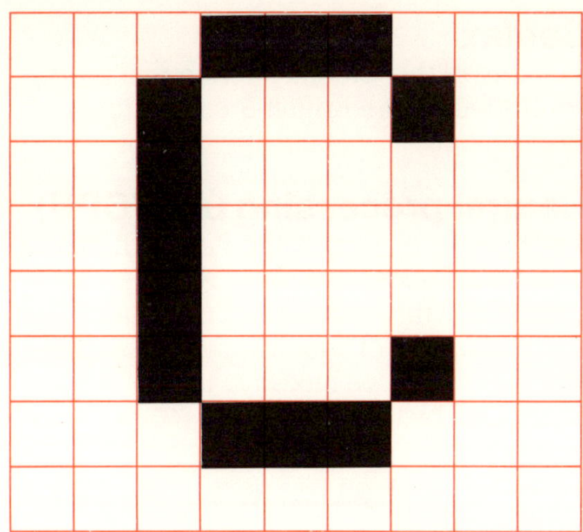

CAD/CAM

Computer **A**ided **D**esign/**C**omputer **A**ided **M**anufacture. Using the computer for designing, developing and producing a wide variety of things, from electronic circuits to car bodies and skyscrapers.

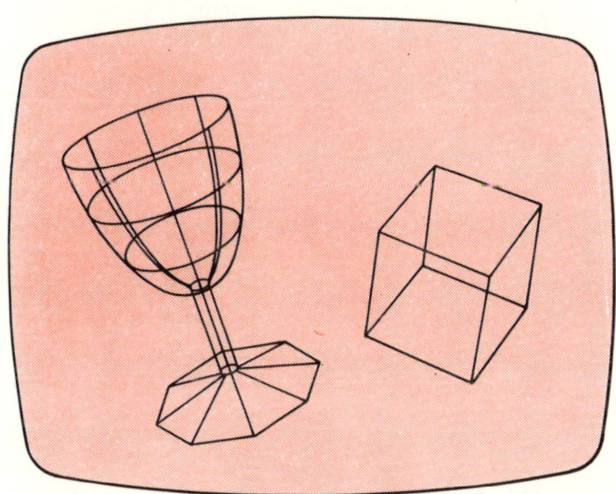

CAI/CAL/CBT/CML (and others)

Computer **A**ided (or Assisted) **I**nstruction *or* **L**earning. The computer acts as a book, blackboard or projector.

Computer **B**ased **T**raining. The special qualities of the computer are used to improve what is being done.

Computer **M**anaged **L**earning. The computer assists the user by controlling what is to be done next, after checking the results of what has already been done.

Capacity

The amount of **data** that can be held by a computer or on tape or disk. Usually measured in **byte**s or **kilo**bytes (K), it gives an indication of how many **characters** can be stored. Microcomputers range in capacity from 2K to 64K or more, floppy **disk**s from 100K to 1000K, and hard disks at least 100 times more.

Card punch

Tool for making holes in computer cards as a means of storing data. The data can later be passed to a computer by a **card reader**. If used **on-line** the holes are punched in positions signalled by a computer; **off-line** they are punched by an operator.

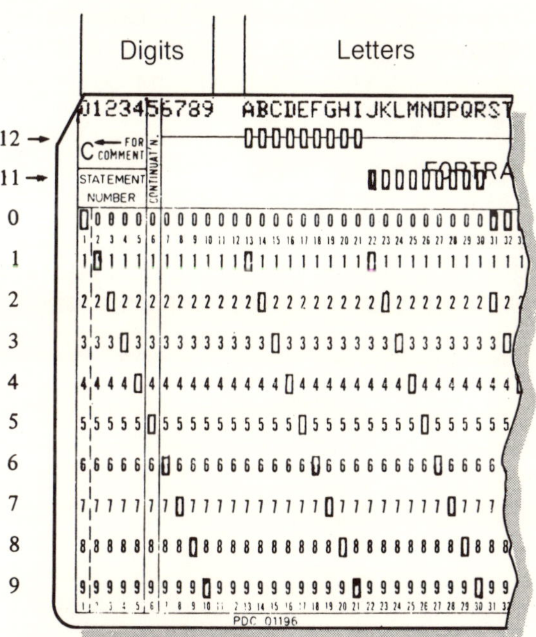

Card reader

Machine that senses where the holes have been made by a **card punch**, or where marks have been put if a **mark sense card** reader, and translates the data into signals that the computer will understand and accept.

Carriage return
Key which on a typewriter returns the carriage carrying the paper to its starting position, ready for a new line to be typed. **Return** key on a computer keyboard also allows the user to start a new line but at the same time it transfers data from the keyboard **buffer** to the computer's main memory.

Cassette recorder
A machine that may be used with a microcomputer to store **data** on magnetic tape held in a protective cover or cassette. Data stored on tape can be loaded back into the computer's memory when required. See also **baud**.

Cassette tape
Used with **microcomputer**s, a cheap form of magnetic storage for which a **cassette recorder** is required. A C10 (ten-minute) tape will hold two 30K programs. See **capacity**.

Cathode ray tube
The normal television picture tube, also used for **VDU**s. A beam of electrons, from a 'gun', is controlled by an electronic lens to produce a picture on the front of the tube.

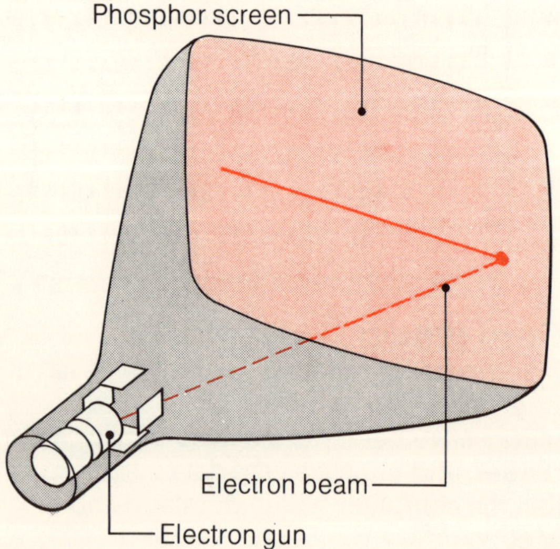

Ceefax
The part of the **teletext** service that is controlled by the British Broadcasting Corporation.

Central processing unit (CPU)
The main part of any computer, with its own **immediate access store**, an **ALU** and a **control unit** that oversees all the other units. All movements of data within the computer and other devices linked to it are controlled by this unit.

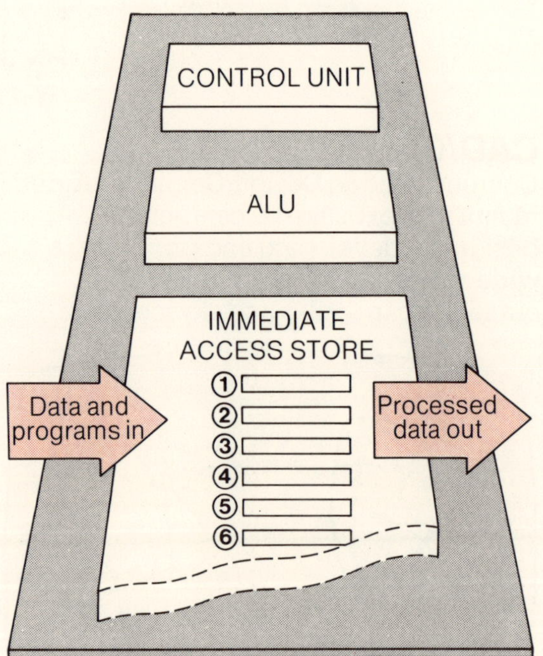

Centronics interface
One of many, this **parallel interface** is an accepted way of passing signals between computer and printer, or other device, if parallel transmission is required.

Channel
The path that data follows within a computer, and to or from a **peripheral**; *or* part of the sound **statement** in a program for computers that can be instructed to make sounds.

Character
Any number, letter, punctuation mark, special sign or shape that can be made by a computer, either on screen or paper.

Character code
Within any computer coding system, such as **ASCII**, each character is represented uniquely, by its own code. Different computers, however, including those that are used in other countries, may employ any one of several different character codes. See also **compatible**.

Character recognition
A method to enable a computer to accept as data printed text or letters, figures and symbols that a person might write. See **OCR/OMR** and **MICR**.

Character set
All those **character**s that a computer has been designed or programmed to work with. Usually includes digits 0 to 9, letters of a selected alphabet, punctuation marks and other such symbols. May also include characters that the user can define.

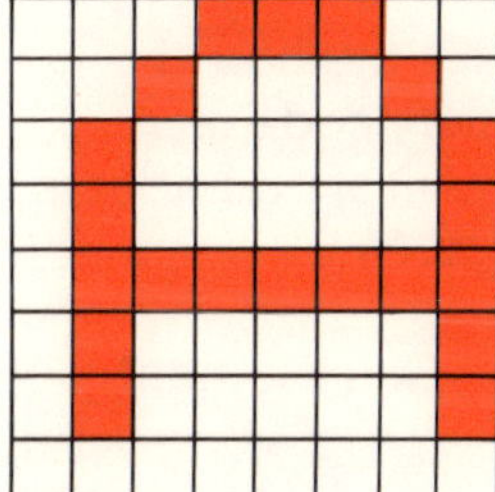

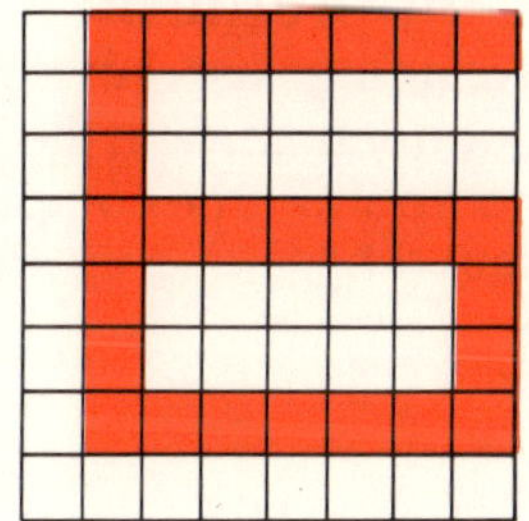

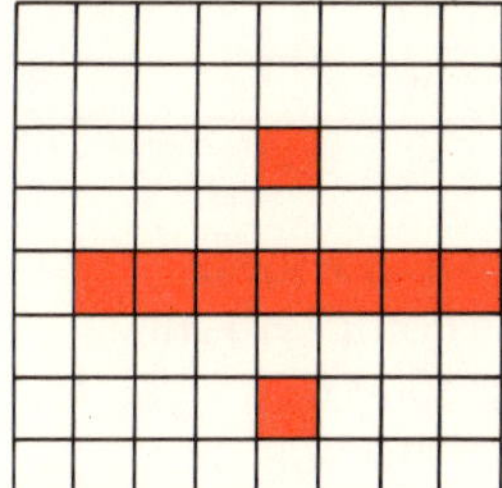

Chart recorder
An instrument for making marks on paper, such as the line of a graph, that can be computer linked and controlled. As the paper passes through, the recorder's pen moves sideways. Sometimes the pen is fixed and the paper moves in two directions.

Check digit
An extra digit tacked on to the end of a number to enable the computer to check whether, for instance, the number has been correctly typed in at the keyboard. The extra digit can be calculated in many ways, but for the check to be successful the same system must be followed every time. Check digits are used to reduce the possibility of errors, e.g. for coding spare parts for cars or numbering items in a warehouse. For example, multiply each digit by its 'position value' and divide by 11. The remainder is the check digit.

e.g. Original number is 475 and
↑↑↑
position values are 321.
3×4=12. 2×7=14. 1×5=5. 12+14+5=31.
31 divided by 11 is 2, remainder 9. So the number used is 4759, where 9 is the check digit.

If any digit is wrong or not in the right place, the computer will not accept it.

Chip
The popular name for 'integrated circuit'. See **IC**.

Circuit
A system of electrical parts joined together to make a conductive path for electricity and perform a particular task. The circuit is said to be 'closed' when an electrical current can flow around it, and 'open' when it cannot.

CLEAR
A **command** that tells the computer to forget what is stored in certain parts of its memory. Can also be used with other commands to clear the **screen** of text or graphics.

Clock
An electronic timing device that sends out regular pulses to keep all the computer's operations in step. Can also be used to time happenings within a computer, or intervals between receiving data from outside.

Coaxial cable
A combination of two or more insulated wires that run inside one another. The outer wire is often a mesh that encloses the rest; it is usually earthed. This acts as a shield and allows the other wires to carry electrical signals with very little interference. Used to connect a microcomputer to a television set, for example.

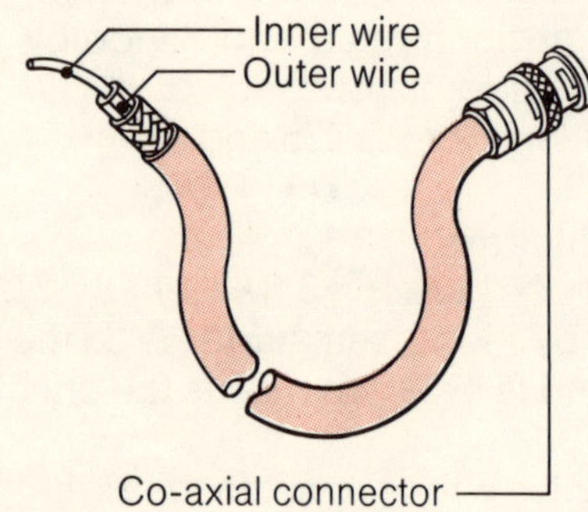

COBOL
COmmon **B**usiness **O**riented **L**anguage. A **high level language** developed in the USA during the late 1950s for commercial and business use. Probably the most widely used of all the programming languages.

Code
The set of instructions that a computer follows when it is running. See also **binary code**, **machine code** and **programming language**.

Colour decoder
An electronic device that changes **digital** signals such as those from a computer into a form that adds **background** and **foreground** colours to the screen.

COMAL
COMmon **A**lgorithmic **L**anguage. A **high level language** developed in Denmark in 1973, which allows the user to write structured programs easily. See also **structured programming**.

Command
Any word that is recognized by the computer as an **instruction** to do something e.g. **Clear**, **List**, **Load**, **Print**, **Run**.

Compatible
When two things are 'friendly' enough to be able to work together they are compatible. Computers are compatible with each other or with **peripherals** if they can use the same data.

Compiler
A **program** that changes a **high level language** program, step by step, into a **machine code** program that has several instructions for each step. The machine code program runs faster as it is directly understood by the computer.

Complement
A number used in a clever method of subtraction. With the **binary code** of computing, the complement of a number is found by 'filling up' the zeros.

Number	Complement
0101	1010
1001	0110
100	011

This chart shows 'one's complement' – adding the number to its complement always produces 1s, e.g. 100+011=111. It is also known as 'flipping the bits' or 'negation'.

For the method of subtraction see **two's complement**.

Computer

A machine, controlled by a **program** stored in its **memory**, that accepts **data** as **input**, works upon it as instructed and **output**s the results. Computers fall roughly into three groups, according to their memory size, speed and power. Starting with the largest, they are **mainframe**s, which are used by big companies, **minicomputer**s used for specific business tasks, and **microcomputer**s, which include all general-purpose 'home' computers.

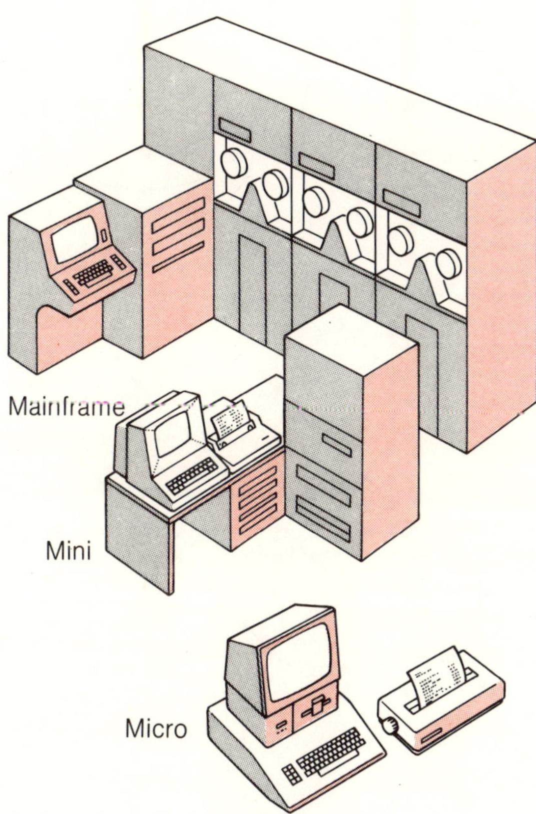

Computer Aided Instruction
Computer Assisted Learning
Computer Based Training
Computer Managed Learning

see **CAI/CAL/CBT/CML**.

Computer bureau

An office or firm that will do computer work for others outside the firm. This might be to provide computing power or to assist with the writing of programs or an **application package**. Very useful to firms who do not have the time or money or staff to do it themselves.

Concatenation

The joining or chaining together of sets of characters, or strings, often under **program** control. For example, the computer might combine the string "HELLO" with another, "MARY", when Mary's password is typed.

Concertina fold paper

Special paper designed to run easily through a **printer**. The paper is very long, and divided into pages by perforations across for easy separation after printing. This allows the paper to fold and lie flat for boxing and carrying, and to be fed to the printer straight from the box.

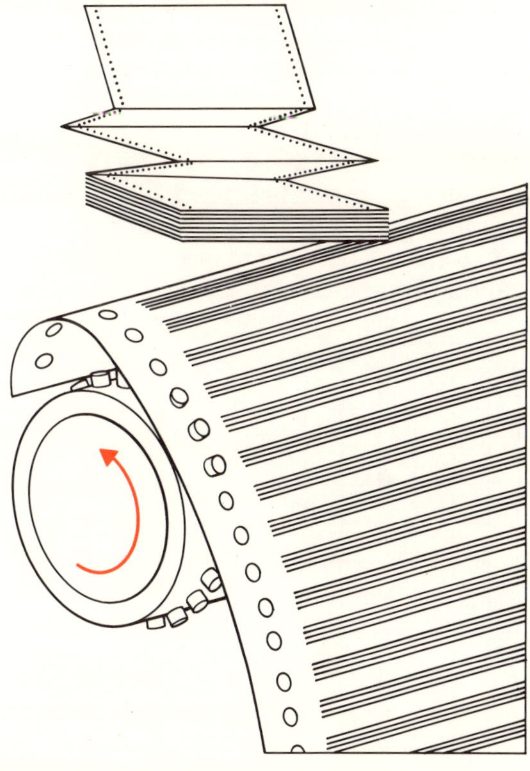

Console
Usually consists of a screen (**VDU**) and **keyboard** linked to a computer. It enables the operator to put messages or **data** into the computer, and/or get messages out.

Continuous stationery
Long lengths of paper very often pre-printed with business forms such as delivery notes, invoices, cheques or adhesive labels, and usually with sprocket holes along the edges for driving the paper through a **printer**. Mostly **concertina fold paper** but also available in rolls.

Control character
A coded instruction from the computer to a **peripheral** telling it to do a particular thing like Start or Stop, for instance, or print something on the screen or on paper. Also used in **word processing** to control the layout of letters and documents.

Control unit
The part of the **central processing unit** that makes the computer carry out each program **instruction** in the correct order.

Co-ordinates
'Grid' references that can be used to specify a point on the screen, like on a graph or map, e.g. 5 spaces in from the left and 8 spaces down from the top. Often called 'X and Y co-ordinates', they can be absolute, i.e. from a fixed point, or relative, meaning that the move starts from the point reached with the previous move.

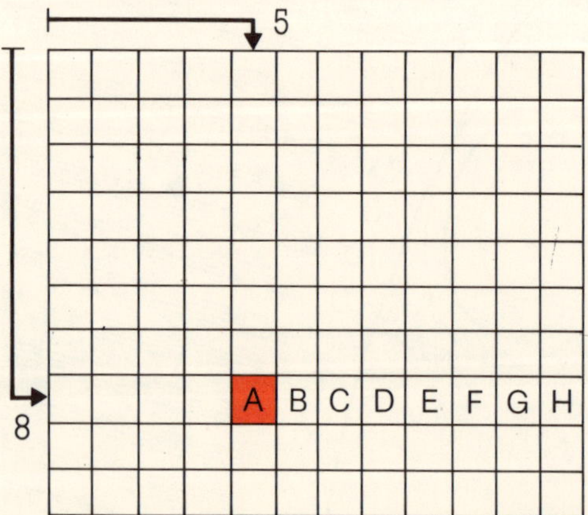

Core store
The main **memory**, or store, of a computer, originally made up of small rings, that can be magnetized to hold **data**. See **ferrite core**. Also describes **semiconductor** memories used in **microcomputers**.

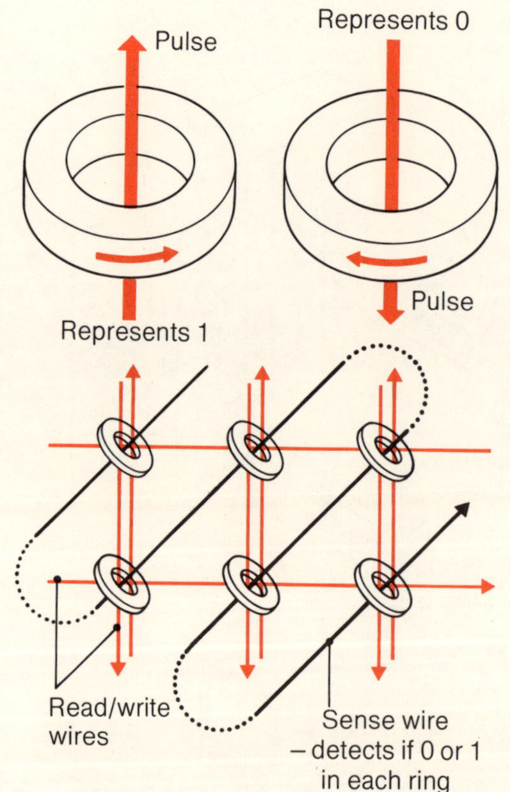

Counter
Counting device. If used to count things (**punched cards** etc.), it is mechanical. More often it is the computer's electronic **register** that checks, for instance, the number of times a step has been repeated in the program.

CP/M
Control Program for Microcomputers. An **operating system** used by some microcomputers, and written specially for those using the Z80 family of **microprocessor**s.

cps
Characters per second. A measure of the rate at which a printer can work. This may be under 50 cps for top quality results from a **daisywheel printer**, 100 upwards for a **dot matrix printer**. **Line printer**s and **ink-jet printer**s are more usually measured in pages per minute.

CPU
See **central processing unit**.

Crash
As might be expected, the word used to say that everything has come to a stop, usually because of an unknown **bug**.

Critical path
A way of planning a project in small steps or sections so that a check can be kept on progress. Very important if time limits are to be set, and often used by computer **programmer**s when working as a team.

CRT
See **cathode ray tube**.

Cursor
A mark, sometimes flashing, that shows where the next piece of information will become visible on the screen. As it does so, the cursor moves on to the next position.

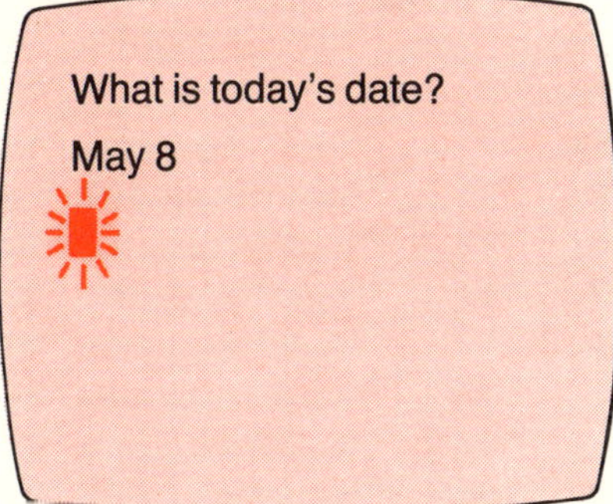

Cybernetics
The theory or study of the similarities between computer control systems and the nervous system of human beings.

Daisywheel printer
A printer whose **print head** consists of a **character set** at the ends of spokes of a rimless wheel, resembling petals on a daisy. The wheel spins to bring the appropriate character into position before striking and inking the paper. Used to produce top quality printed copy. The wheels can be easily changed when worn, or to give different type-faces or character sets.

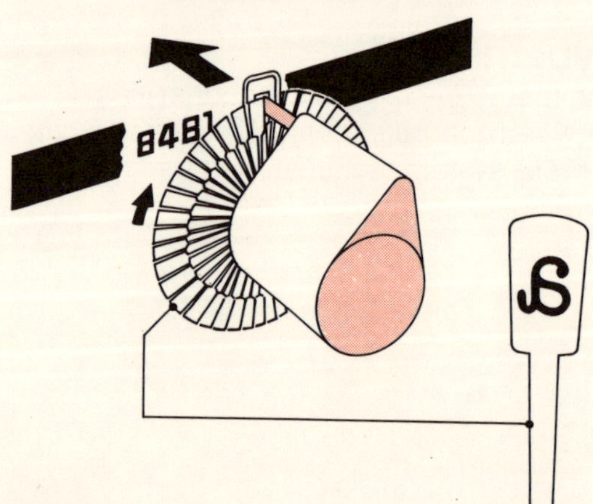

Data
Any coding that can be accepted, stored, processed and output by a computer. It may be numbers or other **characters** or program **instructions** and only becomes **information** when meaningful to people.

Database
A collection of **data** arranged and stored so that items can be selected in different ways by different **program**s. A telephone directory stored as a database might, for example, allow all the people called Brown to be selected by one program, and all those living in house number 15 by another. Large databases can be brought up to date regularly by one user for the benefit of other users. A collection of databases is known as a databank.

Data bus
Inside the computer, the set of wires, or route, along which **data** travels in **byte**s, to and from the **microprocessor**. For a microcomputer having 8-bit bytes the data bus has eight lines in and eight lines out. See also **address bus**.

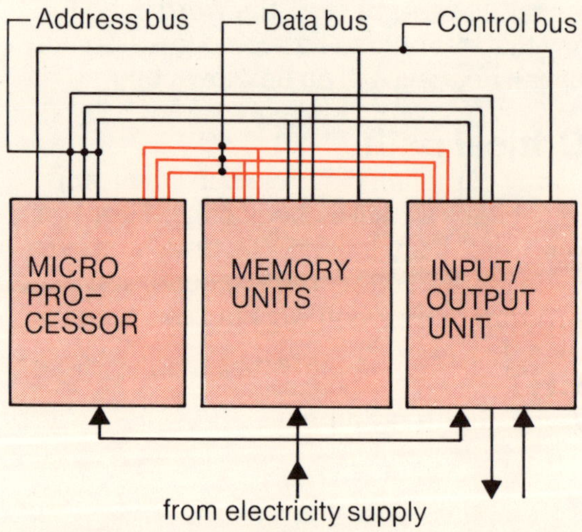

Data processing
The collecting of **data**, working on it, and **output**ting the results. All of which a computer can do with great speed and accuracy.

Data transfer
Moving **data** automatically from one computer to another, or to and from a distant data-collection **terminal** by telephone, radio or cable.

Debugging
Tracing errors (**bugs**) in programs, and correcting them. **Syntax** errors will stop the program running; **logic** errors give false results. Testing and debugging are very necessary to avoid a **crash**.

Decimal
'In tens', the way we usually count and do sums, using the digits 0 to 9. After 9 we start again with 1 in the next column on the left, and begin the first column again with 0. And so on, each time moving one column to the left.

Decision box
A box, usually diamond shaped, that is used in a **flowchart**, to show where a conditional (yes/no) **branch** may happen.

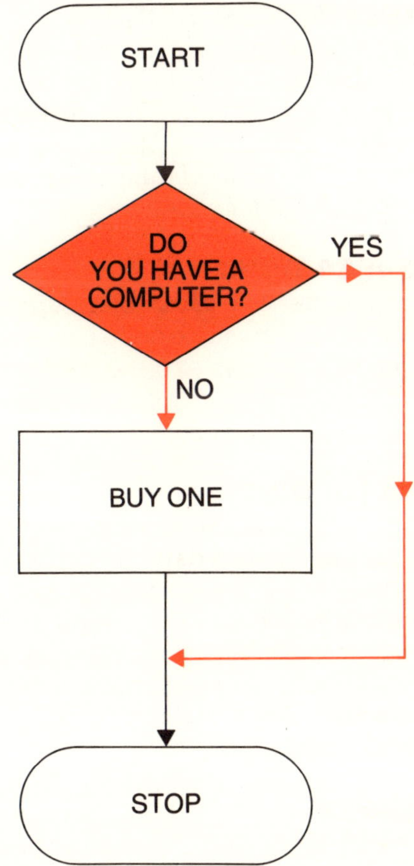

Decoder
Changes coded data to another **code**, to make the data more understandable to a computer or its operator.

Dedicated computer
An electronic device specially programmed to carry out a single task or series of tasks, such as controlling a domestic appliance or working the dashboard display in a motor car. Sometimes part of a **system** for performing more complicated tasks, like map-making, using the signals from satellites.

Default
A safeguard written into a program to prevent the computer from waiting and doing nothing, if, for instance, the user fails to supply data. A default **instruction** or a default value will enable the computer to know what to do in such cases. For example, if the computer asks 'How many spaces do you want for each Name and Address on your List?', and the user presses the return key without supplying any data, the program should give default values of say, 25 for the name and four lines of 20, 15, 15 and 9, for the address and postcode.

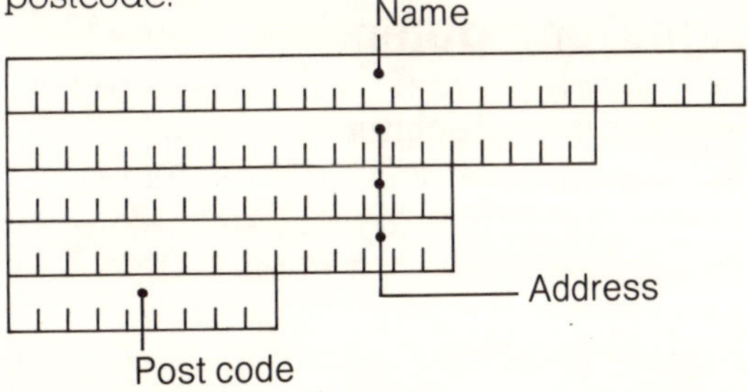

Delay loop
A **subroutine** or **procedure** in a program that allows a wait either for a fixed time, or until a certain event happens. This event could be something the operator does, such as pressing a key, or be a signal from a **peripheral**. A fixed delay may be used to allow the operator time to read something on the screen.

Demodulator
An electronic component that removes the carrier wave, added in **modulation**, which signals need to help them travel long distances, leaving just the signal to be fed into the receiving computer or **terminal**.

Descenders
The little tails, on some **lower case** letters, that go below the line on which they appear, e.g. g, j, p, q, y. Some **dot matrix printers** cannot make true descenders, and print them within the normal line space.

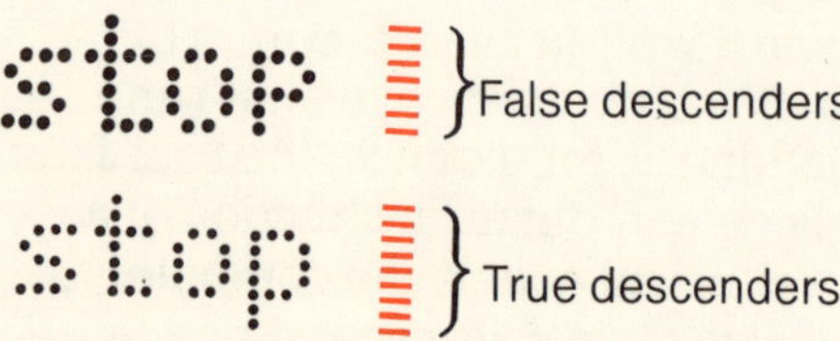

Digit
One of the numbers 0 to 9 inclusive, from which larger numbers are normally made up, e.g. 4835 has four digits. Computers regard digits as data, along with all other characters. See also **binary code**.

Digital computer
A computer that works with data stored in **binary code**. A **decoder** or an **A to D converter** may be needed to change original data into its digital form, before being passed to the computer.

Digital plotter
An electronic instrument for drawing graphs according to data received from a computer. The program calculates the relevant **co-ordinates**, and passes them to the plotter direct.

Digitizer
An **A to D converter**, often used with a **graphics tablet** to convert the position of the pen on the tablet into digital **data** that can be passed to the computer for immediate use, or stored in its memory for future recall.

DIN plugs
A series of connectors with pins arranged in accordance with standards laid down by the German Standards Authority, and accepted internationally.

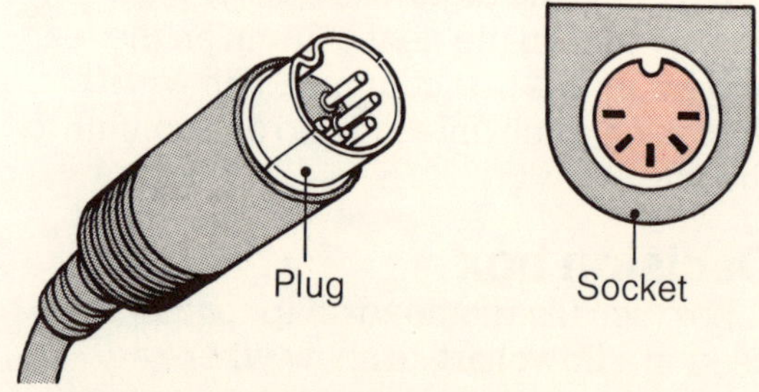

Direct access memory
A form of memory that allows each item of data to be found without having to read through other data first. **Disk**, **diskette**, and **core store** are all examples of this type of memory. Often called **random access memory** (**RAM** for short).

Disassembler
The opposite of an **assembler**. A program for translating **machine code** into **assembly language**, so that an experienced programmer can study it more easily and make changes or spot errors.

Disk (or disc)
A thin, circular plate with a magnetic coating upon which **data** can be stored ('written') or retrieved ('read') using a **disk drive** unit connected to a computer. The data is stored in **binary code** on concentric, circular tracks, and each track is divided into **sectors**. See also **floppy disk** and **hard disk**.

Diskette
A small flexible **disk**. Also called **floppy disk**, or just floppy.

Disk drive

The unit that spins the **disk**s and moves the **read/write head**s across them in response to signals received from the computer. **Disk**s can be 8 inch (20cm), $5\frac{1}{4}$ inch (13cm) or about 3 inch (8cm) in diameter and single or double sided. **Floppy disk**s are driven singly; **hard disk**s often come and are driven in packs, with each disk having its own read/write head or heads.

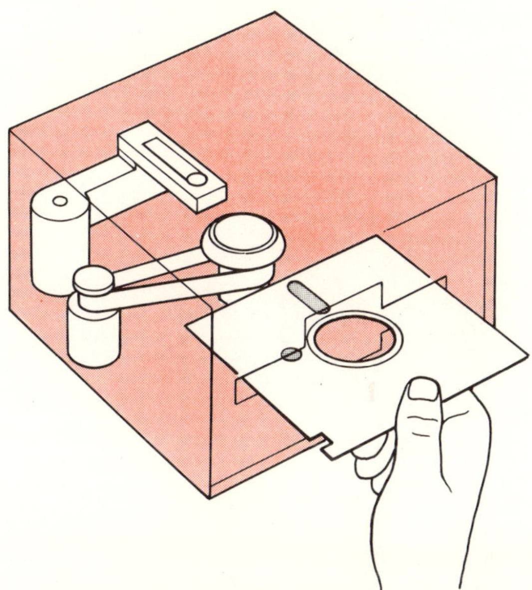

Disk operating system (DOS)

The program, sometimes supplied by the manufacturer in **read only memory (ROM)**, that controls the **disk drive** and the passing of signals and data to and from a computer.

Display

What is shown on the computer screen. May be **text** or **graphics** or both.

Documentation

The necessary instructions, explanations, diagrams and charts, that go with any **program**, **application**s **package** or machine to help the operator check that everything is working as planned. Good documentation also assists in other ways, particularly if a program or package needs to be altered to bring it up to date.

Document reader

A machine that senses marks made on forms and, under program control, produces **data** related to the positions of the marks. For example, the multiple choice (A, B, C, D or E) answer sheets used in examinations. Here the student marks the chosen letter in black pencil for each question and after the document is machine read a computer can work out the number of correct answers from the data.

DOS

See **disk operating system**.

Dot matrix printer

A printer that forms letters and other characters on paper using dots made by needles striking through an inked ribbon. As the print head travels across the paper, seven, nine (or sometimes many more) needles, arranged in a vertical row, are selectively struck. These machines can often print in different styles, sizes and shades, in response to a **control character** sent from the computer.

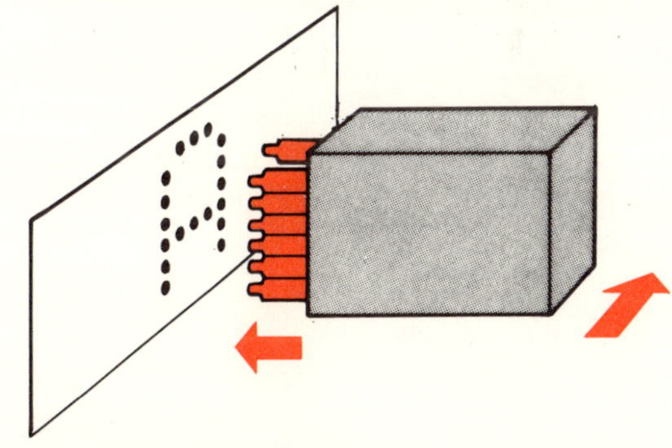

Double density

Doubling the quantity of data stored on **disk**. This can be achieved by doubling the number of tracks or by sending the data faster and in a different **format** so that twice as much is stored in each **sector**.

Downloading
When a small computer system accepts, or downloads data from larger computers and **databases** (like taking information from a large blackboard onto a piece of paper). Such data may travel via any combination of telephone, cable, radio or television. See **Ceefax** and **Prestel**.

Dry run
To test 'by hand' a program or **procedure** that will later be run on a computer. To make sure that they perform only as expected, they are tested with both good and false **data**.

D to A converter
Changes digital signals to analogue. The reverse of **A to D converter**.

Dump
To copy to a **backing store** or other **peripheral**, whatever is in all or part of the computer's memory.

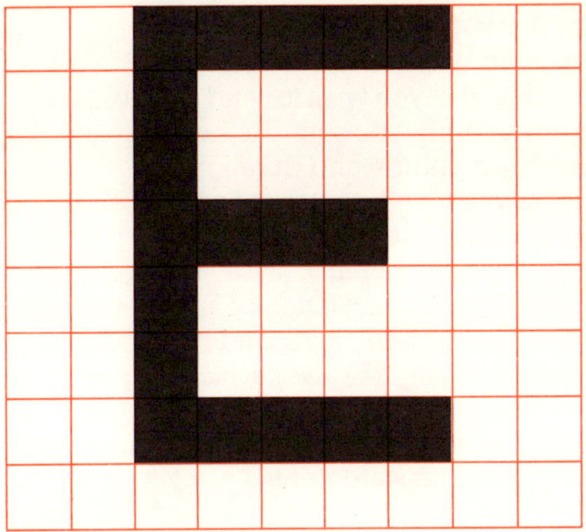

Edge connector

A 'plug' formed by taking the conducting paths of a printed circuit board (**PCB**) to the edge, making possible a connection to a matching socket.

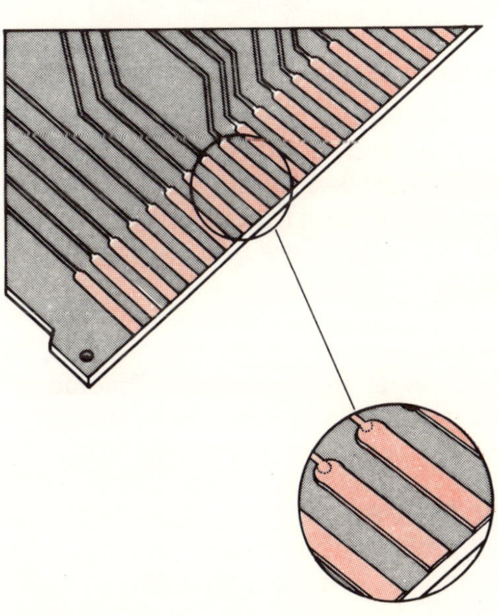

Edit

Change or improve a **program** or the arrangement of **data**. Editing is done before the program is next run. See also **text editor**.

Eight bit

The length of the group of **bit**s that the computer can act upon as a unit. It has come to be accepted as one **byte**. This 'bit length' is called a word, though in bigger or more powerful computers a word can be 16- or 32-bit.

Electronic mail

A method of sending data from one place to another, anywhere in the world, using telephone wires, radio waves, optical fibre cable or satellite. At the receiving end a **terminal** can either output the data to a printer or hold it in memory until it is needed. Replies can be sent in the same manner saving time, postage and paper. See also **telecom**s.

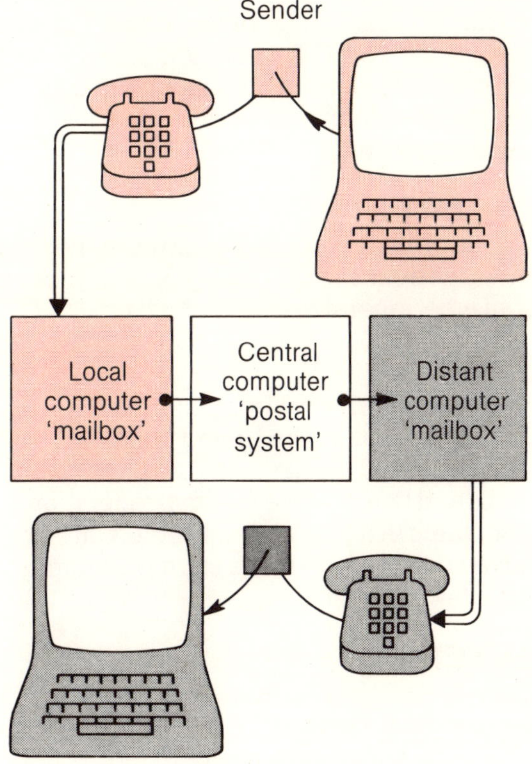

Electronic office
An office that uses the minimum amount of paper. Instead, all memos, letters and reports are passed between people by electronic means. These include computers as well as wires, cables, radio and satellites for communicating at a distance. See also **electronic mail** and **telecoms**.

Electrostatic printer
A printer in which the paper becomes electrostatically charged so that a fine ink dust is attracted to it which hardens when heated and forms the desired characters.

Encoder
An electronic device that changes data in one form into the coded form needed for the next process. For instance, the computer keyboard normally changes the character pressed into **binary code**. Those used by the Post Office change the postcode keyed in into the magnetic dots that are used to mark the envelopes for electronic sorting.

End mark
A **control character** used to indicate the end of a stream of data being passed to or from a peripheral.

ENIAC
Electronic **N**umerical **I**ntegrator **A**nd **C**alculator. Built in the United States in 1946, and used to calculate the ranges of shells and bombs. Like the **first generation computers** that followed, it used electronic **valves** but was not able to store programs, just a few numbers.

ENTER key
May also be labelled 'Ret' or 'Return' on the computer keyboard. Anything keyed in is held in a **buffer** until the operator presses this key, when it then becomes available to the **operating system** or to the program being run.

Envelope
In computer sound production, holds all the data that you wish to send. This tells the computer about a sound to be made, its pitch, amplitude and duration. A description of the sound of a musical note, for instance, would need to (1) start with the time it was first heard, (2) say how long until it was at its loudest (attack phase), and then (3) how long until the sound finished (decay phase), (4) give its highest pitch (frequency) and its lowest pitch, and (5) the time between them. All this would go into the envelope **statement**.

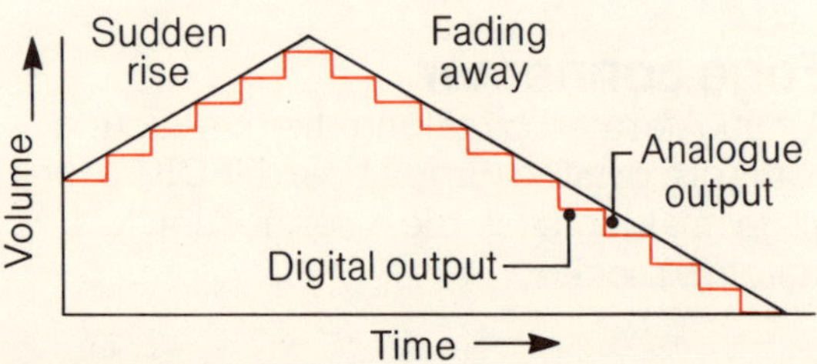

EPROM
Erasable **P**rogrammable **R**ead **O**nly **M**emory. A **solid state** memory that can be erased by a process such as exposure to ultra-violet light and rewritten with new data or instructions as a new **read only memory**.

Erase
Replace data stored in a section of **memory** or **backing store** with the code for 'nothing is stored in here'.

Error message
A message shown on the screen when something goes wrong or everything stops (see **crash**). Can be the simple statement 'Error' or a description of the error saying in which part of the program it occured.

ESCAPE key
On a computer keyboard, key that stops a **program** while it is running, but does not

usually change the program or any stored data. On many computers it can be programmed to do other things, such as move to another part of the program.

Exchangeable disk storage
A **disk drive** unit comprising six or more disks stacked together in a dust-free container. The unit can be changed easily, quickly and safely. Used with **mainframe computers**.

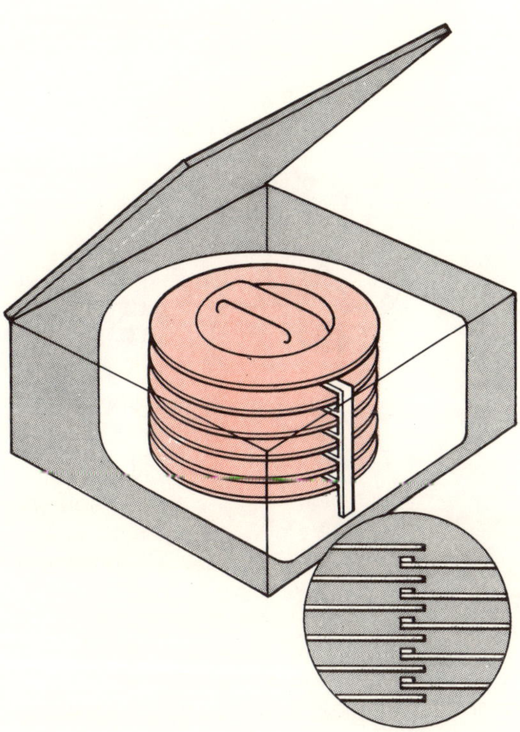

Execute
Do as instructed; that is, carry out a **command** or **routine**, or a complete program.

Expansion port
Any socket on the outside of a computer through which an additional processor, extra memory or a **peripheral** can be connected.

Expert systems
A computer package that will enable beginners to gain access to the knowledge and reasoning of experts. In the future these will operate so fast and have such large memories that using them will be like communicating with a friend.

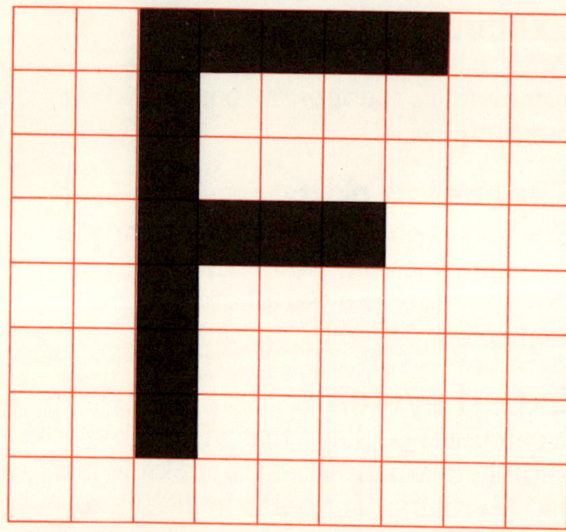

Fail safe
A **system**, or **peripheral**, that stops itself whenever a fault occurs. It does so by following a **procedure** that makes sure there is no damage to program or data.

Fanfold paper
Computer printout paper, made with perforations or creases across, that unfolds and folds up again before and after passing through a printer. See also **concertina fold paper** and **continuous stationery**.

Feasibility study
Assessment of a project before it is started, to find the best possible way of completing it, or even if it really needs doing at all. Often things such as cost, time, and staff training need to be considered.

Ferrite core
A non-**volatile memory**, made up of pinhead-size rings, wired together, that can be magnetized anti-clockwise or clockwise to give the **bits** 1 and 0. Used in great quantities for the **core store** of some large computers.

Fibre optics
The transmission of light along a perspex or glass hair-thin fibre, which has an inner and outer layer with highly polished surfaces. Light entering one end of the inner fibre travels through with very little loss of energy as it is repeatedly reflected from the sides, even when following curves. Electrical signals from a computer are converted into pulses of light that are focused onto the fibre by a glass lens. **Modulation** of the light beam gives interference-free transmission of data, as light is not affected by magnetic or electric activity.

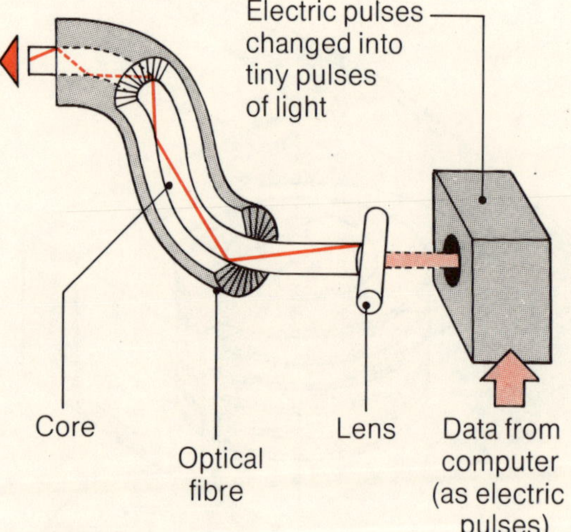

Field
Part of a record, holding one complete piece of information. For a class of schoolchildren each record might list each person's
(1) Family name
(2) First name
(3) House name or number
(4) Street name
(5) Town
(6) Postcode
The quickest way, then, to find out, for instance, how many children live in the same street would be to look at 'field' 4 of each record. This is one way of storing data, with each record having fields and a collection of records making a **file**.

Fifth generation computers
Advanced computers available from 1990 onwards which will operate 30 times faster than the best **fourth generation computers**. They will offer not only **expert systems**, but also a choice of many **languages** running at the same time and much easier program writing. They will also have much more powerful memories and greater decision-making ability.

File
An organized collection of related records, with its own name, label or **identifier**. See also **field**.

Firmware
In between **hardware** and **software**, usually programs in **read only memory** that have been added to, or plugged into, the computer. Since they are not erased by switching off, they are immediately available, with faster **access time** than any backing store.

First generation computers
The earliest computers, built between 1948 and 1956. They used electronic valves and had a very limited memory. **LEO** and **UNIVAC 1** were among the earliest machines used commercially.

Fixed point arithmetic
Method of storing and using numbers in the computer all of which have the decimal point in the same place. This allows faster calculations than does **floating point arithmetic** but not such big numbers can be handled.

Flag
Signal or indicator that is electrically set or unset (on or off) to remind the computer that certain things have or have not happened during a **program** run. For example: Is each **peripheral** ready for action? Has a **data** stream been received completely and correctly?

Flat bed plotter
Type of **digital plotter** that holds paper and has a pen that can move in any direction, including up and down, under computer control. Can be used to produce drawings, graphs or charts. Colour models have several different coloured pens that are used one at a time.

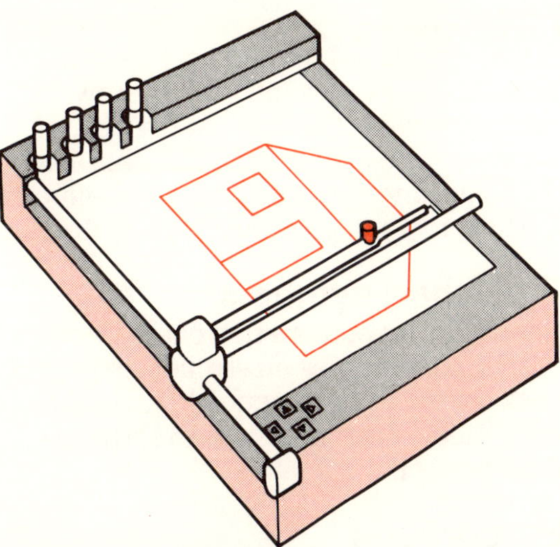

Flight simulator
Program or **dedicated computer** used to train pilots before they fly in the air. The computer alters the instrument readings as the trainee pilot moves the controls. Pictures of airports and runways are projected onto screens as they would appear to a pilot in the air, and the display changes realistically as the instrument readings alter.

Floating point arithmetic
Method of storing numbers in a computer in which the **digits** that make up the number are held separate from the **decimal** point position.

+1346.073 is held as +1346073 and +4.
+0.00327 is held as +327 and −2.
−2.934 is held as −2934 and +1.

This method is much easier to use than **fixed point arithmetic**, and allows both much smaller and much bigger numbers to be stored.

Floppy disk
A flexible **disk** that becomes rigid as it is rotated in a **disk drive**. A cardboard cover, with a slot for the **read/write head**, protects its magnetic coating and the stored data. Also known as diskettes, floppy disks are available as standard floppies, **microfloppies** and **minifloppies**.

Flowchart
A diagram showing the exact flow of a **program** or set of events, that is drawn using 'flowchart symbols'. At the design stage it can be tested using different sets of data, and amended as necessary before the full program is written. See also **dry run**.

Flowchart symbols
The symbols used in a **flowchart**. These consist of boxes of several different shapes, each shape serving a special purpose, that are joined by arrowed lines to show the direction of flow.

Foreground
Colour of the text and/or graphics on a **monitor** or television screen. See also **background**.

Format
The layout or design of something. Examples: the size and shape of a questionnaire form and the position of each line or question; the position of data on a screen or when printed out; the position of tracks and sectors on a **disk**.

Forth
A **high level language** invented in 1969 for faster computer control of equipment. It is much easier to use than **machine code** and allows the user to define new words that are then used as **commands**.

FORTRAN
FORmula **TRAN**slation. A **high level language** developed in the 1950s for solving scientific problems.

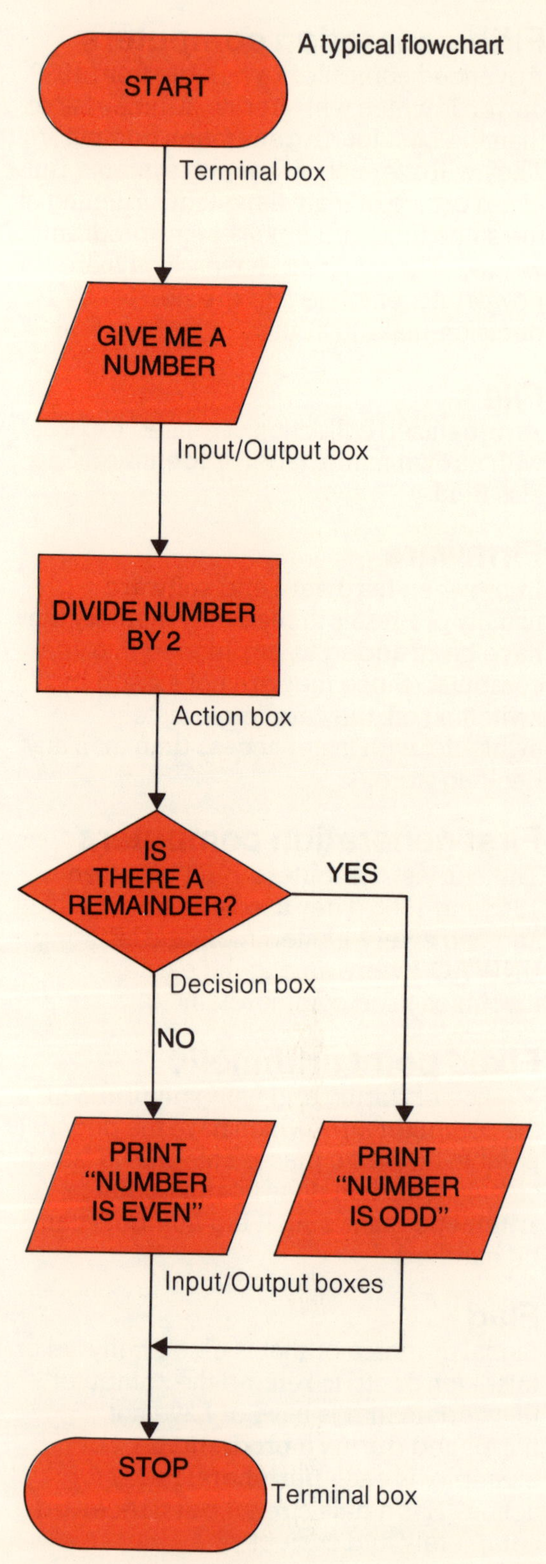

Fourth generation computers
Those computers built during the 1980s with a **capacity** of up to 5000K and speeds of 30 million instructions per second. They were the first to offer **expert systems**.

Frame
Screenful of data, text and/or graphics as on **Prestel**. Also describes one row of holes across a punched paper tape, or one row of **bits** across a magnetic tape.

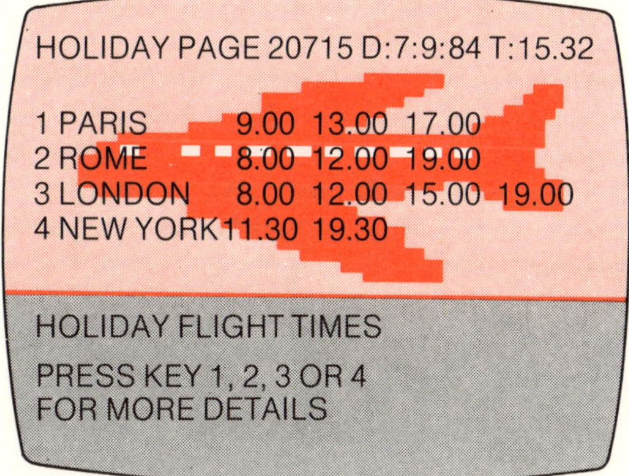

Friction feed
A method of feeding paper into a **printer** or **plotter** in which the paper is gripped between rollers and driven through, instead of using **sprocket holes**.

Full adder
A **logic circuit** for adding numbers in **binary code**. Whereas a **half adder** provides the sum and carry digit when adding just two binary digits, the full adder also includes the carry digit from the next column on the right. It thus adds three binary digits, each time giving the sum and next carry digit.

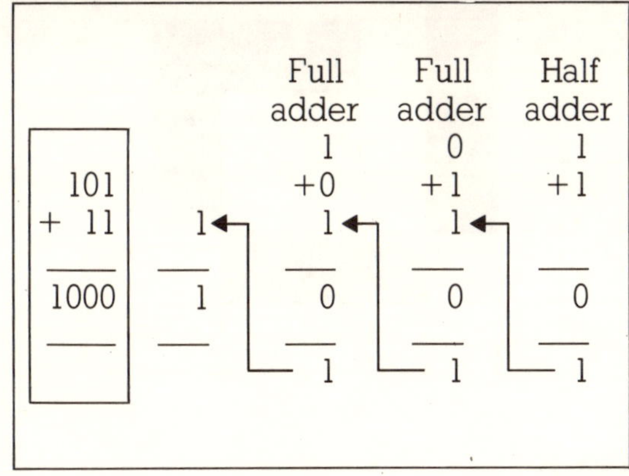

Function code
The first part of a program **instruction**. It tells the computer what has to be done to the data given in the second part.

Function keys
On a computer keyboard, keys that have been programmed by the maker, or can be programmed by the user, to do a task that would normally need two or more keystrokes. For example, using the function key **print**, one not five keystrokes are required. The manufacturer's programmed function keys usually input a **command** or a **keyword**, whereas user-programmed keys can store a complete **procedure** or **subroutine**.

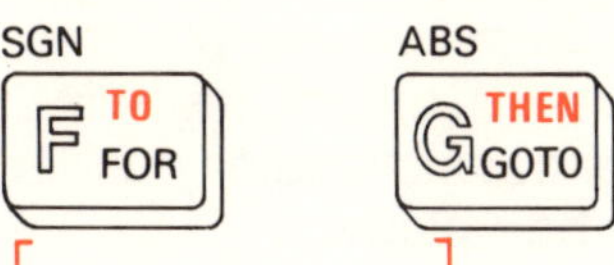

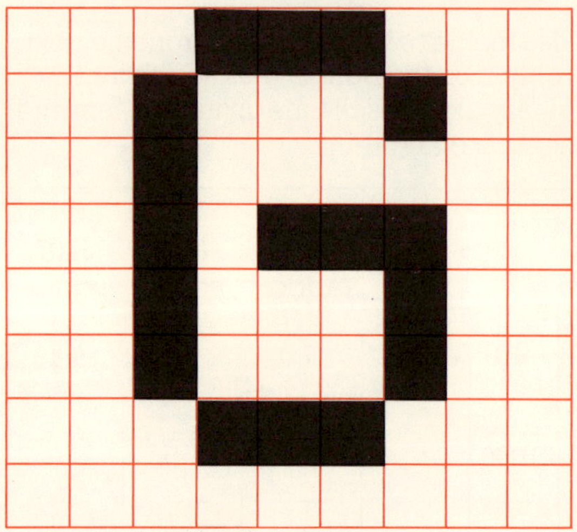

Gate
Inside the computer, an electronic circuit that controls the flow of data. Different gates are used to output a 'pulse' or 'no pulse' (1 or 0) depending on the pattern of pulses received. Some examples are **AND gate**, **NOT gate** and **OR gate**.

Germanium
A chemical element that was used for making **solid state** devices such as **transistor**s, in the 1950s, before silicon was found to be more suitable.

Glitch
A fault which upsets the running of a **program** or spoils the **data** stored on disk or tape.

Graph plotter
A computer **output** device that draws graphs with a pen that moves from side to side as the paper moves along underneath. See also **flat bed plotter**.

Graphical display
Computer **output** that shows charts, drawings, diagrams and text on the screen, in any combination, for educational, business or games purposes. Colours or movement, or both, are often included.

Graphics character set
A set of shapes stored in the computer's memory that can be selected for display on the computer screen. Such shapes may be just large letters of the alphabet or they may represent, say, spaceships and aliens. Often part of the manufacturer's **software**, they can also be created by the user.

Graphics tablet
A computer **input** device that translates into **digital** signals the position and movement of a pen or pointer over a pad, passing such data to a computer for either immediate use or future recall. The data could be used to show the drawing on a screen, or by using a **flat bed plotter** the original could be redrawn on paper at any time.

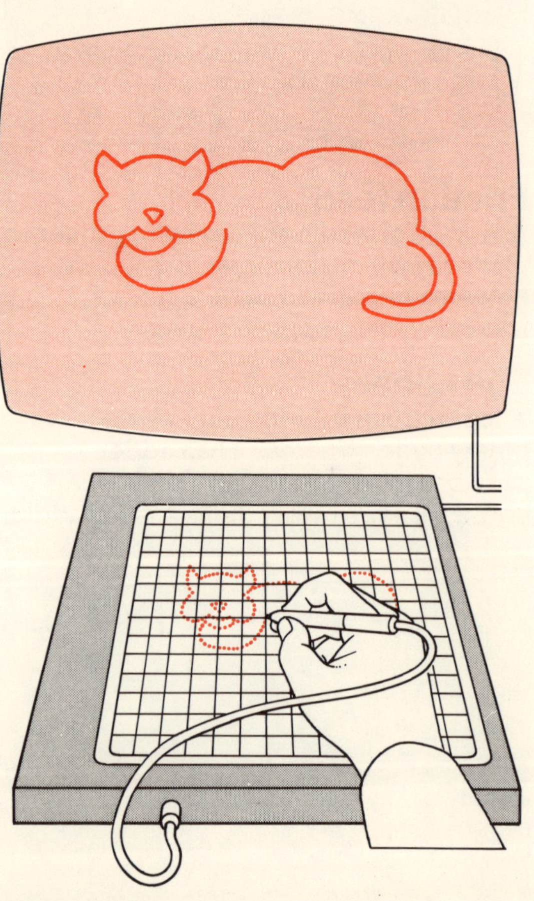

A graphics character set

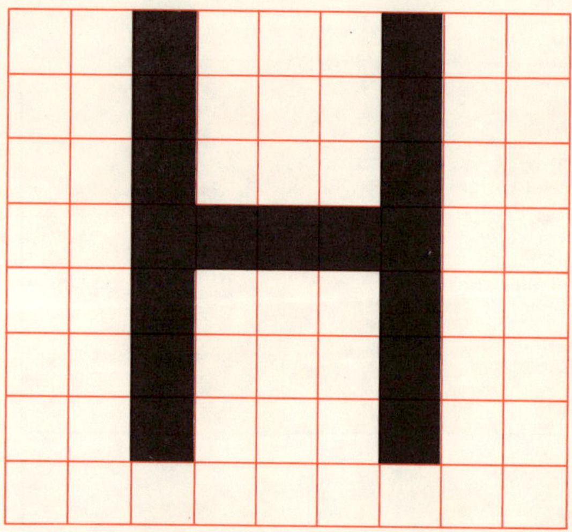

Half adder

A **logic circuit** used to add together two binary digits and give two outputs, the sum and the carry digit. Also known as a two input adder. See **full adder**, **truth table**.

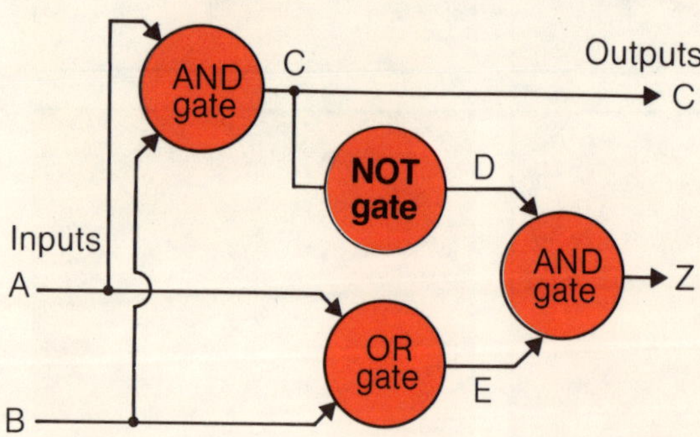

Truth table

Inputs		Output 1			Output 2	Binary addition
A	B	C	D	E	Z	
0	0	0	1	0	0	0+0=0
1	0	0	1	1	1	1+0=1
0	1	0	1	1	1	0+1=1
1	1	1	0	1	0	1+1=10
		Carry Digit			Sum Digit	

Handshake

A signal used to check that a computer and a **peripheral** linked to it are ready and able to transfer data between each other.

Hardcopy

Computer **output** printed on paper.

Hard disks

Rigid magnetic disks for storing computer data and programs. They can normally store more than a **floppy disk** of the same size. See also **disk drive**.

Hard sectored

Type of **disk** that has marks or holes, made during manufacture, to indicate where each **sector** starts. It is these that control the arrangement of data on the disk. See also **soft sectored**.

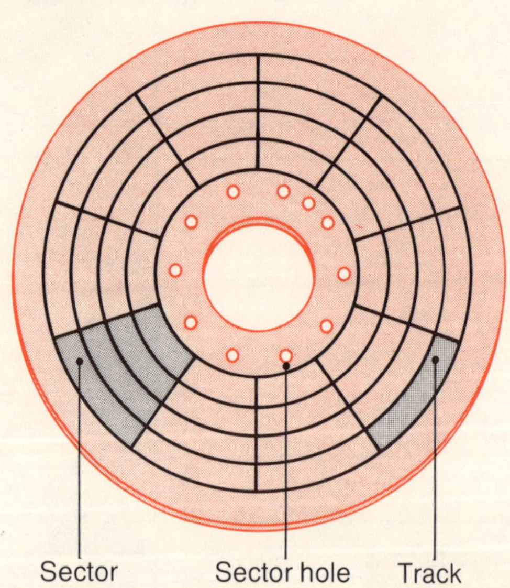

Hardware

Any item of equipment that can go to make up a computer system, e.g. keyboard, screen, printer. See also **software** and **firmware**.

Hardwired logic

Logic built into a silicon chip or electronic **circuit** that is fixed at the time of manufacture, and cannot be altered later. See also **logic circuit**.

Header
A block of **data** holding an **identifier** for the rest of the blocks of data that are to follow. The header may also hold control data to make sure that the blocks are correctly loaded into the computer.

Hexadecimal notation
Notation for counting in sixteens, using the digits 0 to 9 followed by the letters A, B, C, D, E, F to represent the numbers 10 to 15. Called hex for short. **Binary code** needs a four-digit store for any decimal value 0 to 9 (1001=hex 9). But if one is using four binary digits for each number, it makes sense to work in 16s, i.e. from 0000 to 1111. (1111=hex F=15). Counting in sixteens is thus more 'natural' for computers, and hex allows us to remember patterns of binary digits more easily.

High level language
A computer programming language made up of instructions that, with some training, you can understand, but a computer cannot. Common examples include **BASIC** and **Pascal**. Before the computer can execute the program this has to be translated into a language that the computer can recognize and act upon directly. Some high level language programs can be run through a **compiler**, and the resulting **object code** program, which the computer understands, is the one that is kept for future use. Others are stored in memory and read one line at a time by an **interpreter**, which translates the instruction into **machine code** for the computer to carry out. This is done every time the program is run, and so is usually slower than a 'compiled' program.

High resolution graphics
A graphics display with 300 or more dots across the width of a normal computer screen. Each dot is under the control of the computer and can be 'off' or 'on' and probably in any one of four or more colours. See also **low resolution**.

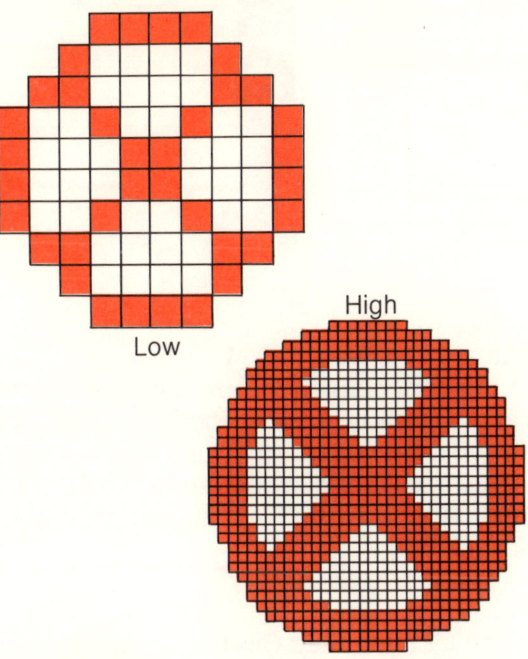

Hollerith
Herman Hollerith (1860–1929), an American who developed a **punched card** reader to assist with the 1900 census by analysing all the details recorded on the cards. His code included the 26 letters of the alphabet, the digits 0 to 9, 27 special characters and a blank. Characters were entered by punching holes in up to three of twelve positions.

Home computer
Generally, a **microcomputer** used at home rather than at work, and for pleasure or education rather than business.

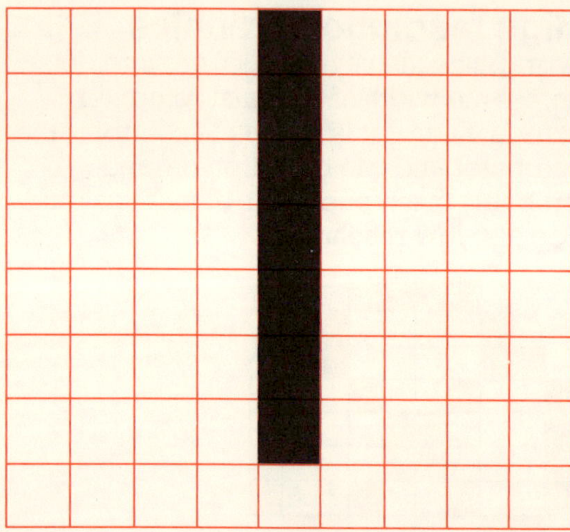

IBM
International **B**usiness **M**achines. An American company that trades world-wide whose methods and practices are often accepted as 'standard'. Thus other companies find it pays to produce **add-ons** and peripherals that can be used with IBM machines.

IC
Short for **Integrated Circuit**. Commonly known as the 'chip'. An electronic circuit having all of its parts formed on a small slice of **semiconductor** material.

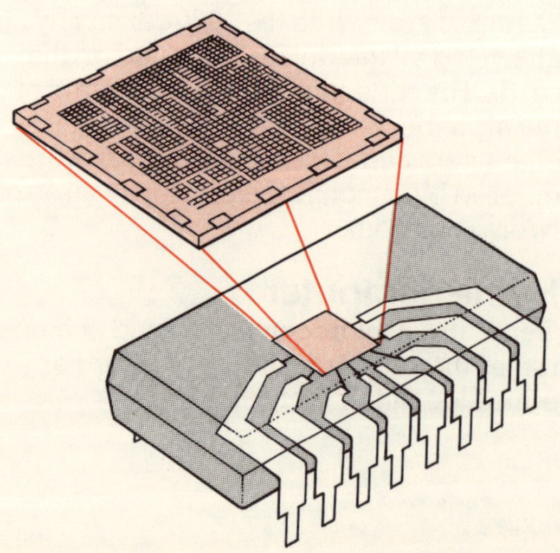

ICL
International **C**omputers **L**imited. A British company in the forefront of computer technology, that trades world-wide.

Identifier
The name or set of characters used by the programmer to label a **file**, or a particular **location** that is storing data.

IEEE
Institute of **E**lectrical and **E**lectronic **E**ngineers. An American organization that assists in setting standard sizes and connections for equipment to make them **compatible**. See also **interface**.

Image processing
The processing of **data** that represents a picture. The computer may (a) extract facts from the picture (e.g. what size is the next item on a conveyor belt), (b) improve the image, as from cameras in space, or (c) just code the data for storing or sending.

Immediate access store
The store, or memory, inside the computer from which data can be retrieved very quickly. Such memories are part of the **central processing unit**; or are addressed directly by the programmer. See **silicon disk**.

Indirect addressing
Method in which the computer goes to one **address** to find the exact address that holds the data it requires. Programmers use this method to fetch or store data in a series of consecutive **location**s, by adding 1 to the value in the first address each time it is accessed. For example, in **machine code** LDA 282A fetches from location 282A an address of where the data is stored.

Informatics
General term for microelectronics and information processing. May be studied, applied or practised.

Information
Data so arranged that it is meaningful to people. For example, an assortment of letters – data – becomes information when organized into words and sentences.

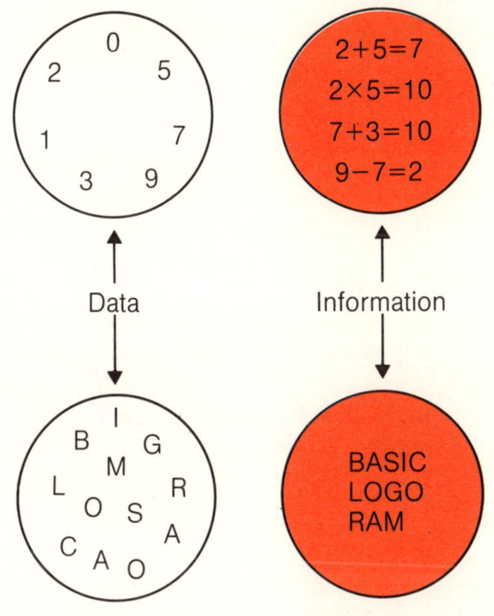

Information retrieval
Getting **information** quickly from any data held in memory. For this, the data has to be stored in a well organized manner, with good indexing. See also **database** and **access time**.

Initialize
To prepare the computer's memory locations that will be used as counters or variables by clearing out any values left from a previous program run, and setting them to zero or other starting values.

Ink-jet printer
A printer that works by firing a fine jet of quick-drying ink at the paper. The ink spray becomes electrically charged as it leaves the jet and passes through an electric field that bends it into the shape of the required character. Can print several hundred characters per second. Type style and size are **program** controlled, allowing printing in foreign languages that do not use the Latin script.

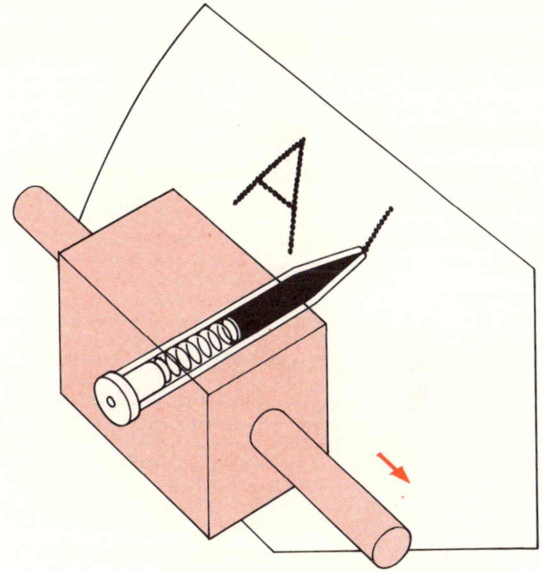

Input
Data going into any computer or **peripheral**. Includes signals from a keyboard, tape recorder, disk drive, joystick or any **transducer** measuring such things as temperature, pressure, light or rotation. One machine's **output** is often another machine's input.

Input buffer
Section of computer memory reserved for temporarily holding data being input until (a) the operator presses the ENTER or RETURN key; (b) a **flag** indicates that the computer is ready to receive data, probably from a **peripheral**. Particularly needed if there is a difference between the transmitting and receiving speeds. Most types of **printers** and **plotters** also have input buffers.

Instruction
The part of a **program** that tells the computer what it should do at that moment. For example,
100 PRINT "What is your name?"
is an instruction (numbered 100) telling the computer to show on the screen the question, What is your name?

Integrated circuit
See IC.

Intelligent terminal
Computer **terminal** that can hold a **program** and carry out its instructions without further help from a central computer; contains **logic circuits** and memory.

Interactive program
A **program** that offers a series of choices, and whose progress depends upon the user's responses. **Videotex** systems such as **Prestel** are interactive in that each **frame** displayed on the computer screen depends upon which keys were pressed by the user. See also **menu**.

Interface
An electronic device that allows two machines to 'face' each other and exchange data. It may be fixed inside one of them, or be free standing, and would have circuits to adjust for any differences in working speeds and **handshake**.

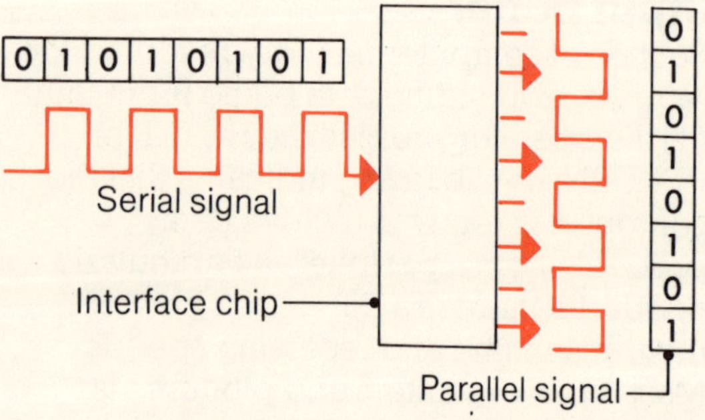

Interpreter
A program, sometimes in **ROM** inside the computer, that takes a **high level language** program one line at a time and changes the instructions into **machine code** for the computer to act upon. See also **compiler**.

Interrupt
Send a signal from a **peripheral** to a computer asking it to stop whatever it is doing and accept data from it. The computer then starts again exactly where it left off. All this is usually done under the control of an interrupt **routine** in the program.

Inverse video
Computer screen display using colours the opposite way round to how they are usually seen. On a black-and-white screen it gives, for example, black characters on a white background.

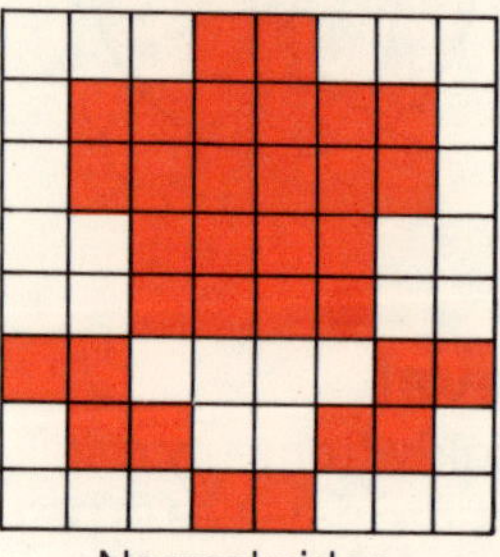
Normal video

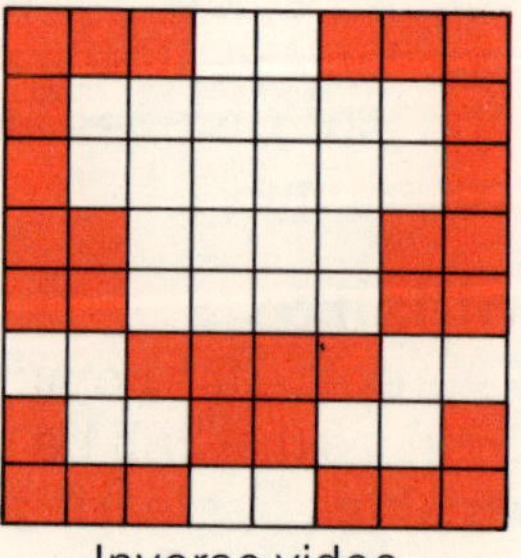
Inverse video

I/O ports
Input/output ports. The connections through which the **input** and **output** data flow to and from the computer. Usually sockets into which **peripherals** are plugged. They are made to certain

standards depending on the number, size and position of the connecting pins, and may have an **interface** attached.

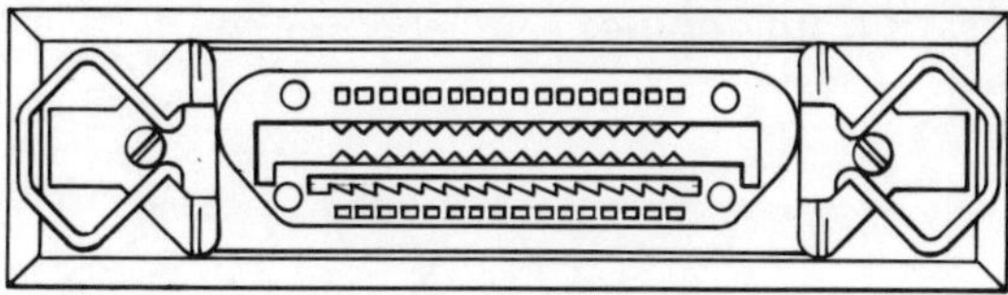

Inverted file

An organized collection of data, or file, that has a 'key' letter or symbol attached to each record to assist with speedier identification. For example, in a file of 'Train details' such a key might be used to show which trains are running late. To find this information the computer would then not need to scan all the records, only the ones with the correct key.

Iteration

Method of solving a problem by getting an approximate answer, and then using this answer to get a more accurate one. The process is repeated over and over until there is very little difference between the answers being obtained. The latest answer is then accepted as the right one. People find this process takes a very long time but computers, because of their speed, have made the method very popular.

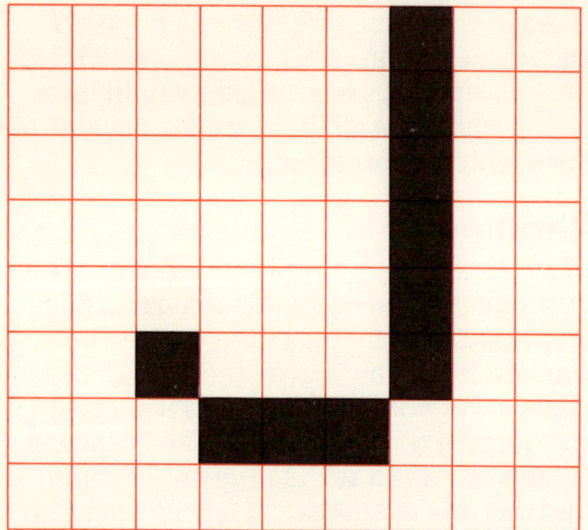

Jack plug
A standard, one-pin plug used for some computer connections. Widely used on tape recorders and headphones.

Jacquard
Joseph Jacquard (1752–1834), a French straw-hatmaker who developed the idea of using holes in **punched card**s to control the mechanical actions of weaving looms. The cards passed over a drum, and weighted control wires were either stopped by the card or went through the holes, so raising the warp threads of the material.

Joystick
A **peripheral** that sends signals to the computer that vary as the stick is moved in any direction. Often used to control movement of an object on the screen, they can be used in pairs for games or competitions. Some have a 'fire button' to control the ejection or shooting of one object from another.

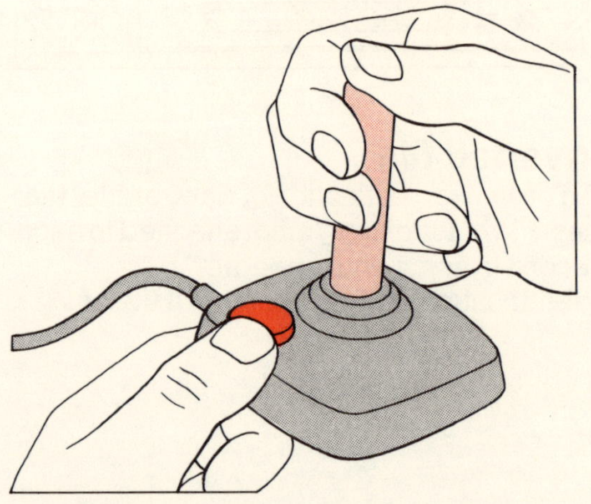

Justify
To even up the margin spacing at the beginning or end of a line of text or figures. Columns of figures are usually right justified, aligning under the units column, and ordinary printing is left justified, as in the main text of this book. Text can be both left and right justified, as in newspapers, by slightly adjusting the spaces between letters and words to fill out lines to the full width.

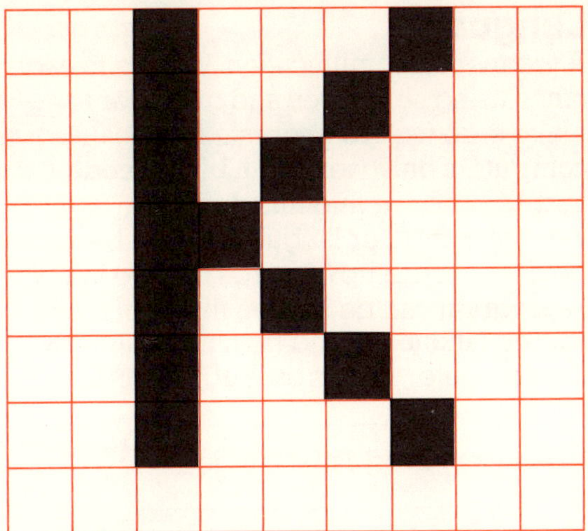

K or Kilo
One thousand in the way we count, but in computer jargon is taken to be 1024 because computers count in 2s (**binary**); 2, 4, 8, 16, 32, 64, 128, 256, 512, 1024. Thus 2 to the power of 10 (2^{10})= 1024= 1K. See also **capacity**.

Keyboard
Any arrangement of keys that when pressed send a code to the next stage of the system. For example, a typewriter sends letters and figures; a **card punch** sends holes in correct places; and a computer keyboard might send **ASCII** code.

Keyword
A word included or placed within data to assist with **information retrieval**. The computer is then able to select items according to the keyword or keywords chosen.

Kimball tag
A small **punched card**, or magnetically striped card, holding coded data. Attached by shops to items, they are removed at the time of sale and used as **input** to a computer for stock control purposes.

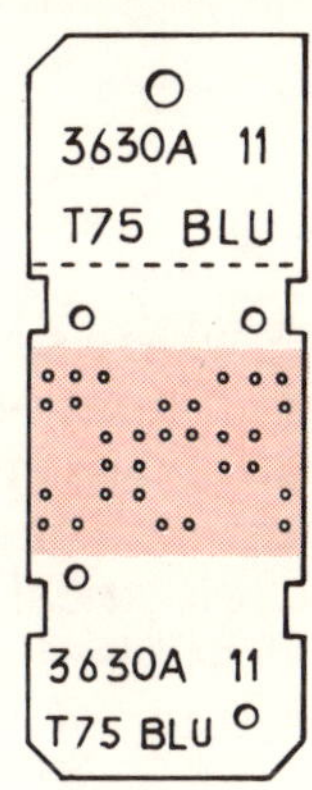

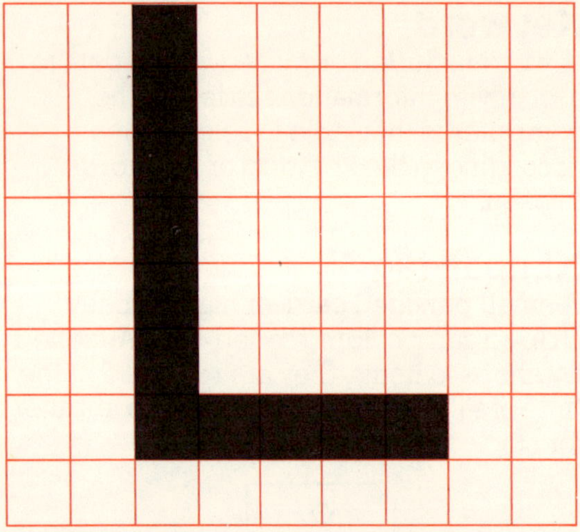

Language

A means of communication. We talk to each other using sentences and grammar to make sure we are understood. Because computers only work with **binary code** (0s and 1s), and we find this difficult to use, various computer languages have been devised, made up of words that we know. A **program** can be written in one of these **source languages** and then translated by the computer into its own **object code**.

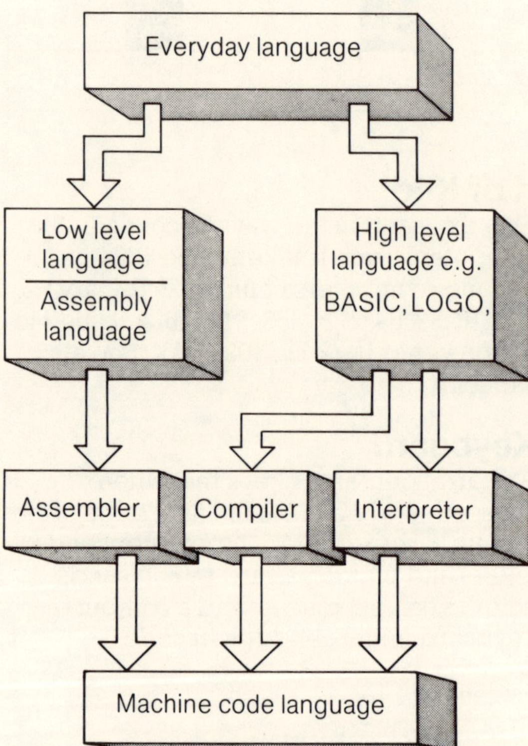

LAN

Local **A**rea **N**etwork where several microcomputers are connected together for the fast exchange of data and the sharing of **peripheral**s like printers and disk drives. Various electrical connection arrangements are possible, such as 'bus', 'ring', 'star' and 'tree/branch'.

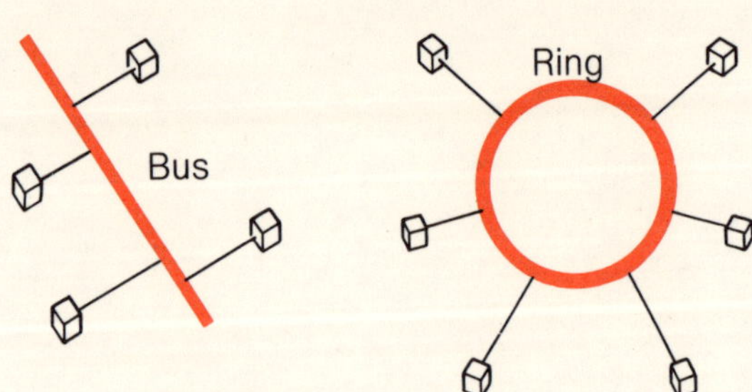

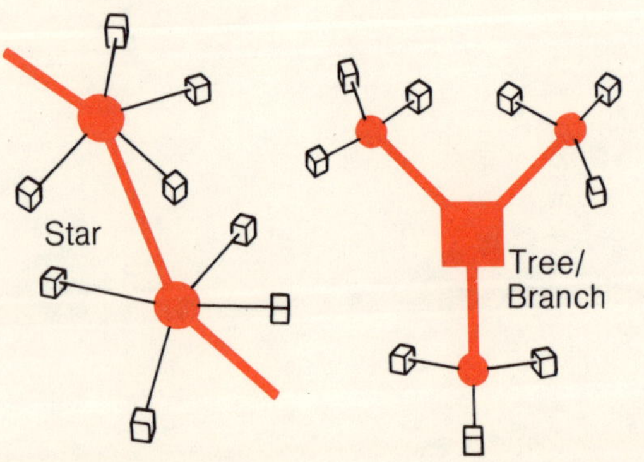

Large scale integration (LSI)

Many **logic gate**s packed onto an **integrated circuit** (chip). Since about 1970 has been taken to mean above 200. The mid-1960s saw Medium Scale Integration (MSI), between 50 and 200 gates per chip. Less than this is SSI (Small Scale Integration). VLSI (Very Large Scale Integration), above 5000, is the present range, but this is still increasing. By 1990, ULSI (U=ultra) will offer over half a million logic gates per chip.

Laser printer
A computer printer that forms a page of print by sending a beam of light onto an electrically charged drum, which then attracts ink to the shape of the projected characters. Prints around 25,000 lines per minute.

LCD
Liquid **C**rystal **D**isplay. **Output** device that forms a character by darkening small sections of the display area, in response to electrical signals received.

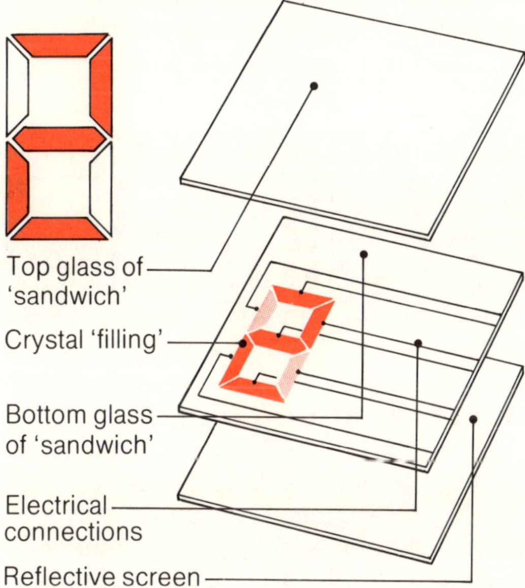

Leibniz
Gottfried Wilhelm von Leibniz (1646–1716), a German philosopher who designed one of the first mechanical calculators that could multiply and divide as well as add and subtract.

LEO
Lyons **E**lectronic **O**ffice. One of the earliest commercial computers (1953), first used by the firm of J. Lyons for payroll and accounting. A **first generation computer**, that was later adopted in the UK by the Inland Revenue and British Rail among others.

Library software
The **program**s and **routine**s made available by the computer manufacturer for users of their equipment. Can also be all programs and routines developed within a company or department and kept for use by its own operators.

Light pen
A light-sensitive instrument that enables the user to draw on a computer-controlled screen. Sections of the picture can be moved or changed in shape, size, position and colour, depending on the program in use at the time. The pen's position is worked out by the computer when the tip detects the spot of light which continuously scans the screen making the picture.

Line feed
An instruction to move to the next line, either on screen, or on paper in a printer. Can be carried out as part of a program, or by pressing a button on the printer or on a keyboard.

Line number
A number telling the computer that the instructions following are part of a **program**. This means that they are not to be carried out immediately but only when the program is run. They are then done in numerical order unless the program instructs differently.

Line printer
A computer printer that prints a complete line by printing all the As, then all the Bs and so on. To print HELLO, it would print the E, then the H, followed by the two Ls and the O.

1. E
2. HE
3. HELL
4. HELLO

It has a revolving print head, with a hammer at each character position across the page. As the correct characters come into position the hammers press the paper on to them. Speeds range between 200 and 2000 lines per minute.

Liquid crystal display
See **LCD**.

Lisp
List **P**rocessing, a **high level language** used particularly in **artificial intelligence** research. It allows more flexibility than traditional computer languages.

LIST
A **command** telling a computer to print on screen or paper, and in **line number** order, the program at present in its memory. Can be a complete listing, or only part of the program.

Listing
Printout of programs, or data, in **line number** or **location** order.

```
3   REM    *** A SAMPLE LISTING***
10  PRINT "INPUT A FARENHEIT TEMPERATURE"
20  PRINT " AND THE COMPUTER WILL OUTPUT"
30  PRINT " ITS FARENHEIT EQUIVALENT"
40  PRINT " ENTER 0 TO FINISH"
100 INPUT "FARENHEIT";F
110 IF F = 0 THEN GOTO 150
120 PRINT " CENTIGRADE EQUIVALENT OF";F;
130 PRINT " IS";(F - 32)*5/9
140 GOTO 100
150 END
```

LOAD
A **command** that tells the computer to store in its memory a program coming from a **backing store**. Can also mean to put a data medium, such as a magnetic tape, into an input device, in this case a tape recorder.

Local area network
See **LAN.**

Location
A place in a computer's memory that stores **data**. Each location has its own **address** number, and the computer can be told to, for example, "Store this data at 1291".

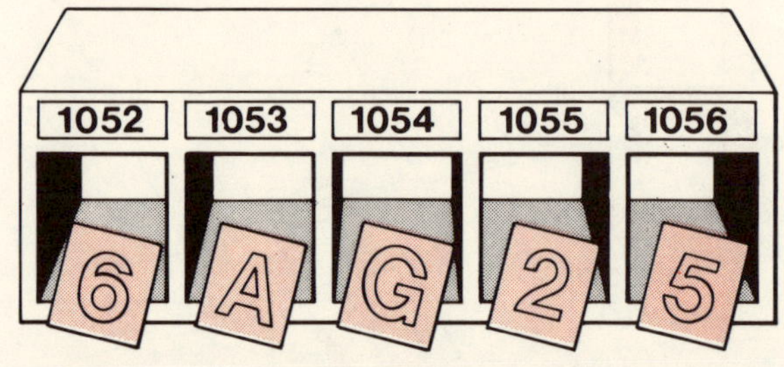

Logic circuit/Logic gate
A logic circuit on a silicon chip is made up of many logic gates. Different types of gate output a pulse of electricity only when certain combinations of pulses are put in. See **AND gate**, **OR gate**, **NOT gate**. **Truth tables** are used to chart the various possibilities of gates and circuits.

Logic seeking
On a **bi-directional printer**, facility that helps speed up printing by not allowing the printhead to travel to the end of a line unnecessarily. For example, if the line of print finished halfway across the page, printing from left to right, the machine would look at the next line to see if there were anything to the right of the printhead's present position. If so, the head would continue across, if not then it would immediately print the next line from right to left.

Log in/out
The correct way of entering or leaving a large computer system when using a **terminal**. Usually involves keying in a personal user number or code. Checks can then be made on who uses it, for how long, and if a charge is to be made.

LOGO
A **high level language**, designed in 1969, to help children, in particular, to learn by experience how to use a computer. It encourages the use of language in a logical and structured way, leading naturally to 'microworlds', in which problems can be solved using a few standard solutions.

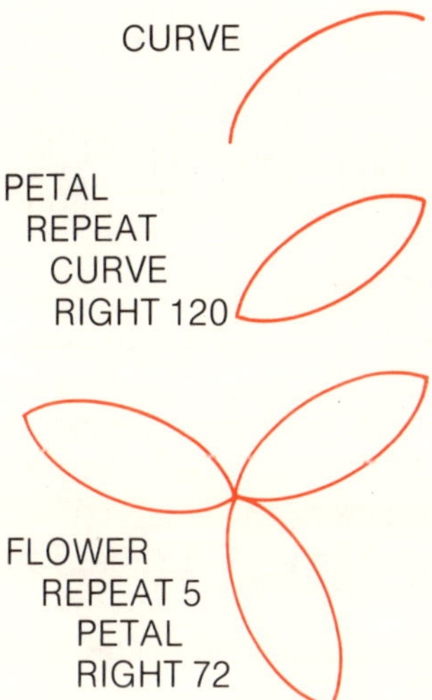

Look-up table
A reference chart. At its simplest could be an ordinary 'times' table as used in school arithmetic. Stored as data in a computer's memory, it would then always be ready for use when needed. Data arranged in this way forms an **array**.

Loop
A section of a **program** that repeats itself over and over again, either for a set number of times, or until a preset condition is met. See also **rogue value**.

Low level language
Normally, a computer language that uses **mnemonics**. Each instruction is translated into a **machine code** instruction that the computer directly understands. Used when speed is important. Can also refer to machine code itself.

Lower case letters
Small letters, not capitals.

Low resolution
Computer screen display in which the eye can usually see the 'build-up' of a picture or graphics character quite easily. Normally, fewer than 300 dots or **pixels** across the width of a normal screen. See also **high resolution graphics**.

LSI
See **large scale integration**.

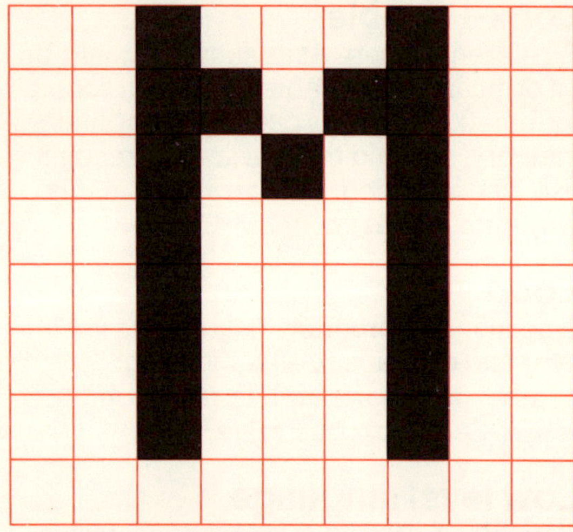

Machine code
A binary (comprising only 0s and 1s), **low level language** which a computer understands. When you write a program in a **high level language** such as BASIC the computer translates this into machine code in order to carry out your instructions. Programs can be written in machine code, though to enable such programs to be written more easily most computer manufacturers offer an **assembly language**. Machine code programs run very fast and are often used in computer games where constantly moving **high resolution graphics** are required.

Machine independent/specific
A **program** or **procedure** that can be used on any computer is said to be machine independent. One that can be used on only one type of computer is machine specific.

Magnetic disk
See **disk**.

Magnetic ink
An ink containing particles of magnetic material used to print numbers and letters that can be read by both people and electronic machines. In a cheque book the number of each cheque is printed in magnetic ink so that the user can read the number and the cheque can be machine-sorted at the bank.

1 2 3 4 5 6
7 8 9 0
A B C D E F G
H I J K L M N
O P Q R S T U
V W X Y Z

Magnetic tape
The most widely used form of **backing store**. Mainframe computers use large reels of tape, microcomputers use cassette tapes. Unlike disk storage, which provides **direct access memory**, it can take several minutes to find an item on tape. Tape is much cheaper than disk, however, and on a commercial scale it also takes up less space.

Mainframe
A large, powerful computer able to process vast amounts of data and do several jobs at once. Such a system has many **terminal**s, some a long way from the computer itself. Strictly speaking, the mainframe is the **central processing unit** of the computer.

Mark sense cards
Computer cards pre-printed with boxes which can be marked with a pencil line. The marks are read by a light detector and the data fed to a computer for processing.

Used by sales people to record orders and by students to answer multiple choice questions.

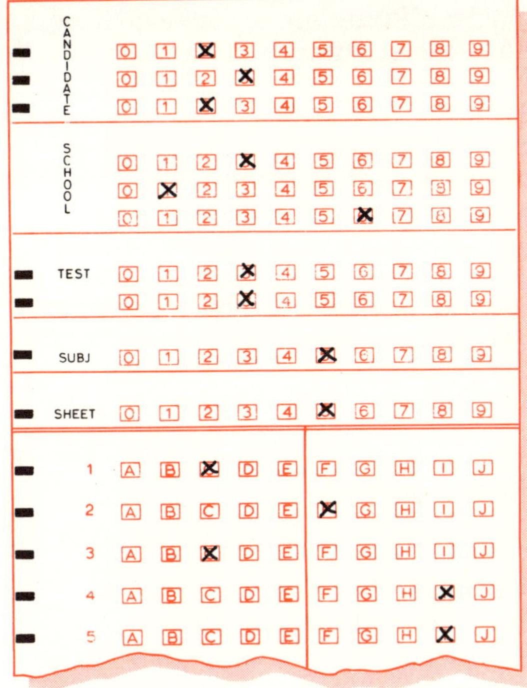

Master file
A computer **file** that holds all the data from which working files are copied for everyday use. Rarely used except when it is being **update**d, though is always available should something go wrong with the working file copies.

Matrix printer
Any printer that forms its characters by printing dots. Speeds of several hundred characters per second are possible. See also **dot matrix printer** and **thermal printer**.

Media
Computing materials used to hold **data**, for example, **continuous stationery**, **magnetic disk**, **paper tape**.

Megabyte
A million **byte**s.

Memory
The computer's internal or main memory, sometimes called the **immediate access store**. It is divided into **RAM** and **ROM** and its capacity is measured in kilo**byte**s, or **K**.

Memory mapping
A method of storing codes for **character**s that are being displayed on the computer screen. Each display position has its own **address** and so the whole screen is 'mapped' in memory.

Menu
A **display** that lists several alternatives and invites the user to choose from them. The alternatives are usually labelled in such a way, say A, B, C, that the user only has to press a single key to choose.

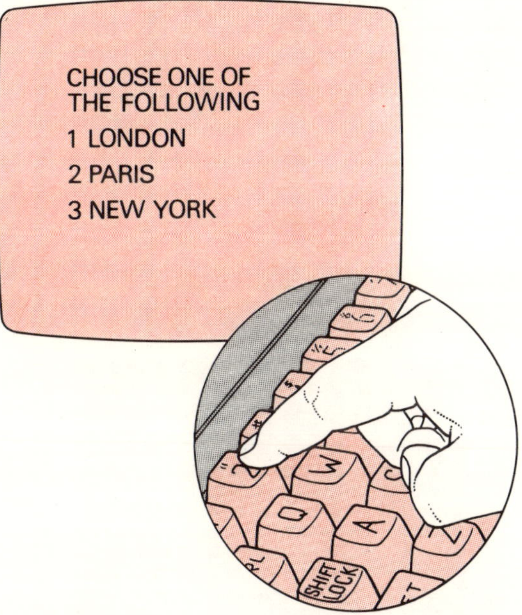

MICR
Magnetic **I**nk **C**haracter **R**ecognition. Used by banks and building societies for automatic sorting of their cheques and forms carrying numbers printed in **magnetic ink**.

Micro
Literally, 'very small'. Commonly used as an abbreviation for **microcomputer**.

Microcomputer
A computer that has a **microprocessor** as its 'brain' or **central processing unit**. The first one was produced in the USA in 1975.

Microdrive
The **backing store** used on computers such as the more expensive Sinclair/Timex machines which is capable of storing 100 **K** or more. It uses a continuous loop of **magnetic tape** and has its own drive unit. Although much faster than a normal cassette it is slower (though cheaper) than a **disk drive**.

Microfiche
A small sheet of film, similar to a large photographic slide, it can hold in miniature form hundreds of pages of print or diagrams. Viewing is done through a special projector. **Output** from a computer can be put directly onto a microfiche or onto microfilm. Used in libraries to store pages of catalogues.

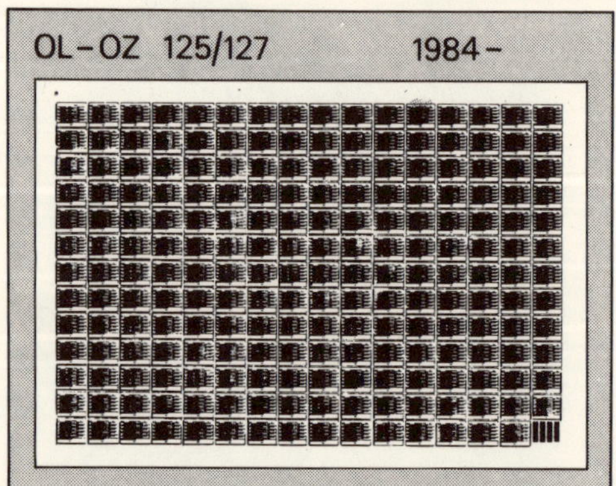

Microfloppy disk
A flexible magnetic disk, usually about 8 centimetres (3 inches) across. Smaller and less used than the **minifloppy**.

Micronet 800
A service that offers its subscribers access to computer software by displaying it on their computer screens. In addition, all the facilities of **Prestel** are available to its users. See also **telesoftware** and **videotex**.

Microprocessor
The **integrated circuit**, or chip, used as the **central processing unit** of a microcomputer. Inside the computer, it can easily be identified as it is likely to be the largest chip on the circuit board and is probably labelled Z80 or 6502. These two 8-**bit** microprocessors handle eight binary digits at a time. Sixteen- and 32-bit machines are also available, which are faster and can handle more data at a time.

Microsecond
One-millionth of a second.

Microwriter
A portable pocket-sized electronic machine, designed for writing, storing and editing text. It has just six keys and is operated with one hand. The text can at a later time be printed or transferred to a **word processor**.

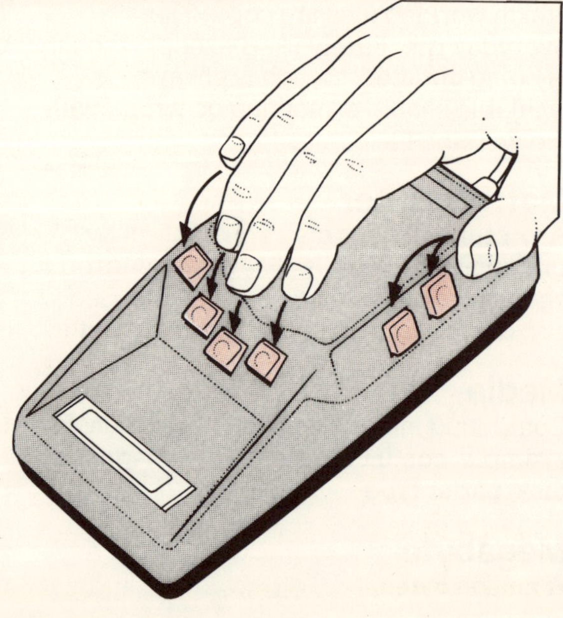

Millisecond
One-thousandth of a second.

Minicomputer
Traditionally, a computer whose size and price came between those of a **mainframe** and a **microcomputer**. With the ever-increasing speed, memory and processing power of microcomputers, together with their **network**ing facilities, the distinction between mini and 'micro' is becoming less clear.

Minifloppy
A 13-centimetre ($5\frac{1}{4}$-inch) diameter **floppy disk**, the most popular disk backing store for microcomputers. Usually has 40 or 80 tracks each with a number of **sector**s, and can hold between 70 **K** (if single-sided) and as much as 700 K. Although they are flexible when held, the disks become quite rigid when rotating at 300 revolutions per minute in their drive unit.

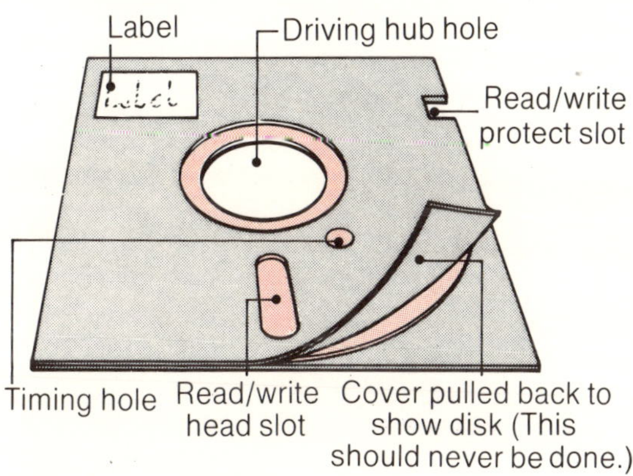

Mnemonics
Abbreviations of English words that can easily be remembered. Normally used for the operating code when writing programs in a **low level language**. For example;
LDA 007
ADD 008
may instruct the computer to load the **accumulator** with the contents of **location** 007 and then add to it the contents of location 008.

Mode
The way in which a computer or its **software** is working. Some microcomputers offer a variety of graphics modes, some various **character** modes, and some a mixture of the two.

Modem
MOdulator/**DEM**odulator. An electronic component that converts digital signals from a computer into **analogue** sound signals so that they can be sent along a telegraph line. Similarly, it changes back, or demodulates, signals it receives. Unlike an **acoustic coupler** it plugs straight into the telephone system. See also **A to D converter**.

Modulation
The changing of digital signals into a series of rapidly-varying, **analogue** sound tones that can be transmitted along a telegraph line.

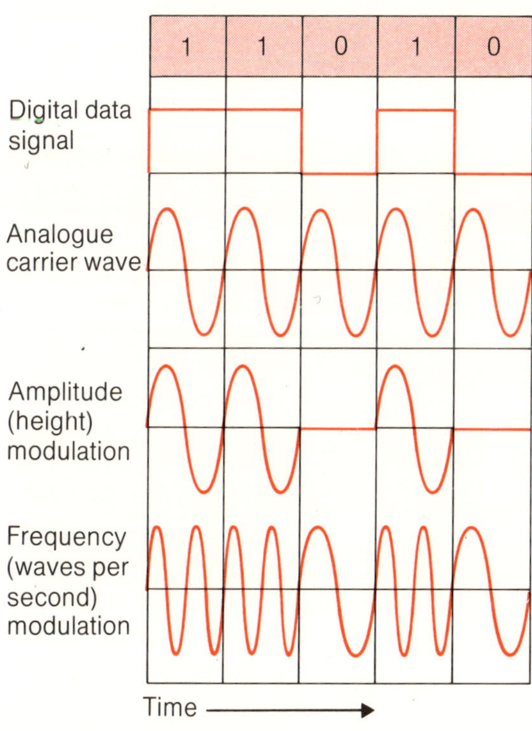

Module
A small part of a **program** that is complete in itself and performs one specific task. In producing a complete program, several modules are joined together in a precise manner. See also **subroutine**.

Monitor
1. A control program that arranges the order of use of various pieces of equipment.
2. A television-like output device or **VDU** that accepts signals from a computer but not the aerial signal used by a normal televison set.

Monochrome
Having only one colour, usually white, on a black screen. See also **inverse video**.

Motherboard
The **printed circuit board** that holds, supports or controls the other boards inside the computer. Generally the circuit board that contains the **microprocessor**.

Mouse
A handheld **input** device resembling a mouse which when moved on a desk-top controls the position of a light **cursor** on the screen. The user selects one of the options in a **menu** displayed by moving the cursor until it is on top of the correct option box and pressing a button on the mouse.

Multi-access system
System that allows many users to have access to one computer at what seems like the same time. For example, the many electronic cash registers in use in a large department store if they are connected to one large computer.

Multiplexor
A device that allows many separate **signal**s to travel to and from a computer along the same path. By switching on and off very quickly, it can route data from, or to, particular wires, each seeming to have a continuous link to the main computer.

Nanosecond
One thousand-millionth (billionth) of a second.

Napier
John Napier (1550–1617), a Scottish mathematician who designed a set of 11 rods with markings which, when put side by side, could be used to do multiplication by just adding. He later invented logarithms, which made multiplication even easier. They, in turn, led to the slide-rule, and then to the calculator, and so to today's computer.

Negation
The reversing of the **bit** value of each bit position for a number in **binary code**. For example:

01011 would become 10100

101 would become 010

This is similar to finding the **complement** of a binary number.

Network
A system that allows many users to share facilities such as **mainframe**s, **printer**s and **backing store**s and to send data to each other although they may be a long distance apart. A local area network, or **LAN**, provides low-cost, reliable and fast communication between microcomputers and peripherals on one site.

Normalize
When using **floating point arithmetic**, this means that every number stored in the computer has the same number of digits after the decimal point.

NOT gate
One of the simplest **logic gate**s used within a computer to control the flow of data. What is output is the opposite of what is input: a pulse seems to change into 'no pulse' and vice-versa. The 'truth table' below charts the results, using 0 to indicate 'no pulse' and 1 for a pulse. A NOT gate is sometimes called an 'invertor'.

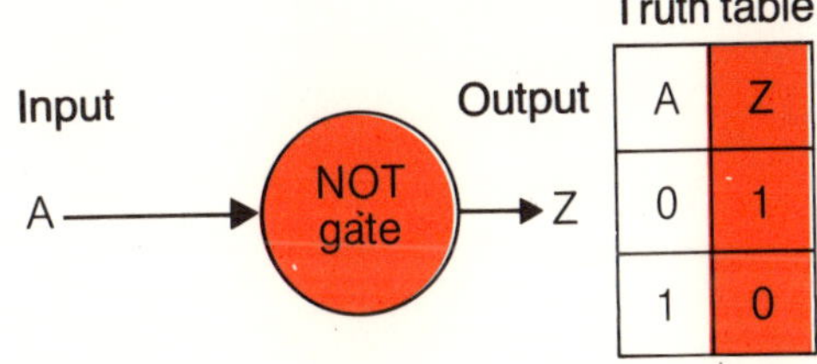

Truth table

A	Z
0	1
1	0

NTSC
National **T**elevision **S**tandard **C**ommittee. One of the three international standards for producing television pictures: NTSC output in the USA, PAL colour in the UK and parts of Western Europe, and SECAM in France. Each standard defines how many lines there are in a **raster scan** and the speed of scanning.

Null string
A **string** having nothing in it; null means 'nothing'. Most likely to be input by the user when just the ENTER or RETURN key is pressed in answer to a question on the screen. The programmer can arrange a **default** input to be taken by the computer when this happens.

Number cruncher
A large computer that has great calculating power rather than data processing ability. Used by financial organizations.

Numeric
Dealing with numbers, whether they are in binary code or octal, decimal or hexadecimal notation.

Numeric keypad
A special input device for the numbers 0 to 9. May also have other keys such as +, −, ×, /, = and ENTER. See also **alphanumeric keyboard**.

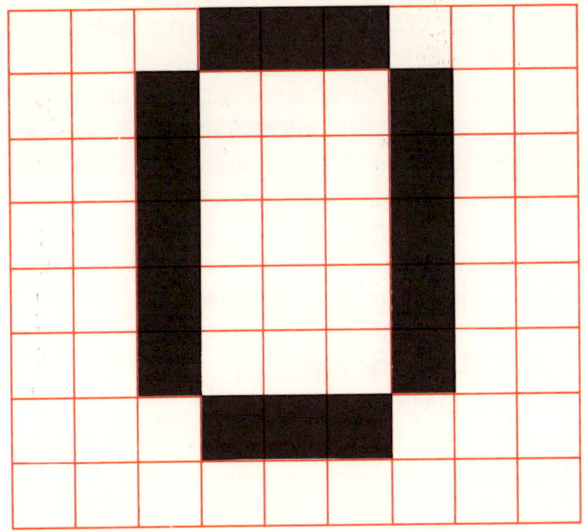

Object code
Code in which an **object program** is produced by the computer. Another name for **machine code**.

Object program
The **machine code** version of a program written in a **source language**. It is produced by an **assembler** or a **compiler**. If written in a 'high level language' such as **BASIC**, the same source program can be compiled several times over to produce different object programs for different computers.

OCR/OMR
Optical **C**haracter **R**eader/**O**ptical **M**ark **R**eader. Light-sensitive devices that can recognize the shape of a **character**, or the position of a mark, on paper, and pass the correctly coded signal to a computer.

ABCDEFGHIJKLM

NOPQRSTUVWXYZ

0123456789.,

{}%?⑀⑂⑁:;=+/$

Octal notation
Counting in eights, using the digits 0 to 7. Useful for remembering numbers that are in **binary code** as each octal digit represents three binary digits. (0=000 and 7=111). Each digit position in a number represents eight times the value of the one to its right.

Binary	Binary in groups of three	Octal	Decimal
101010	(101) (010)	52	42
1100	(001) (100)	14	12
110010.01	(110) (010) (010)	62.2	50.2

One-dimensional array
A list that needs only one **identifier** (number, letter or character) to 'pin-point' the data. For example, in a class list, number 6, say, would represent only one person. If, however there were four classes, there would be four number 6s, and, to be certain of finding the right one, both 'class' and 'number' (**two dimensional array**) would be needed.

One touch entry
Pressing one key to make the computer do something, without needing to press the **ENTER** or RETURN key afterwards. While waiting for the user to press a key such as Y or N (yes or no) the computer continually checks the keyboard. It then acts accordingly as soon as the user presses one of those keys.

ON/OFF line
On line is when any input or output device is directly connected, and ready to transfer data to or from a computer. Off line, data is collected and prepared, ready to be passed when needed.

Op-code/Operand

Every **instruction** given to a computer has to tell it what to do – the operation code or op-code – and where to find the data on which it has to be done – the operand.

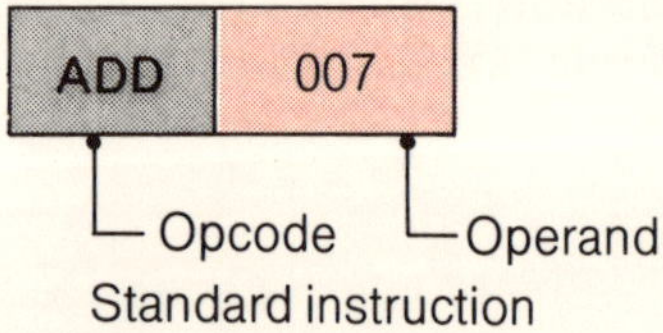

Standard instruction

Operating system

A **program** that has overall control of the running of a computer, making sure that everything happens in the correct order, at the right time and in the proper place.

Optical character reader

See **OCR/OMR.**

Optical disk

A disk that stores data in a digital form for use with audio disk players, video disk players and computer systems. Disks are 'written to' by a laser beam (very powerful light source), which produces tiny pits in the disk's surface. Another type of laser 'reads' the disk. Such disks are robust, long lasting and give fast **access times**.

A 13-centimetre (5-inch) diameter optical disk for a microcomputer would hold several **megabytes**, whereas a commercial 35-centimetre (14-inch) disk could hold several thousand megabytes.

Drive unit

Laser beam

Pits in disk

Optical mark reader

See **OCR/OMR**.

Oracle

The part of the **teletext** service that is controlled by the Independent Broadcasting Authority.

OR gate

One of the **logic gates** used within a computer to control the flow of data. An OR gate will seem to output a pulse if either or both inputs have a pulse. 'Truth tables' are used to chart these results.

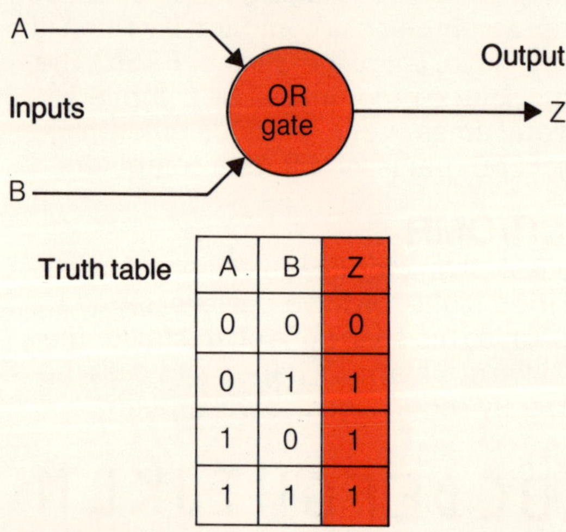

Truth table

A	B	Z
0	0	0
0	1	1
1	0	1
1	1	1

Oscillator

An electronic circuit that provides regular pulses (at least a million per second) which are used to govern the speed of working of a computer. May be part of the **microprocessor** or can be contained on a separate chip.

Output
Broadly, whatever comes out of anything. In computer jargon, used to describe results obtained from a computer (a) in printed form, (b) as screen display, (c) as data flowing to a **peripheral**, or (d) as the results from a peripheral such as a **card punch**, **paper tape** punch or **graph plotter**.

Overflow
The situation arising when the answer to a calculation is too long for the computer to hold. Usually results in a message to the operator and/or a warning **flag** being set within the computer.

Overlay
A way of coping with a program that is too long for the space available in a computer's memory. Parts of the program are brought in as needed, from **backing store**, during the running of the program. Each new section 'rubs out' the previous one and takes its place. See **overwrite**.

Overwrite
To 'rub out' data from memory and replace it with fresh data. (To rub out and *not* replace, is to **erase**.)

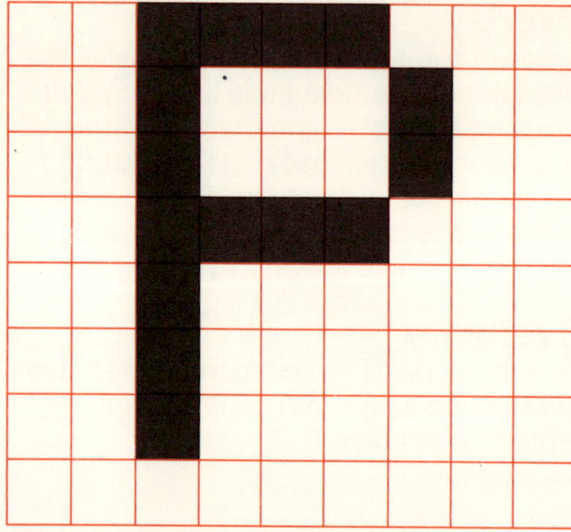

Packet switching
A method of passing data between computers linked together in a **network**. Each 'packet' of data carries a code saying to which computer it has to go, and travels round the network until it reaches the correct one.

Packing density
The number of **bit**s that can be held in a certain length of backing store.

Paddle
A hand-held electronic input device with a rotating knob, which enables the operator to move characters around the screen. Used for playing electronic games.

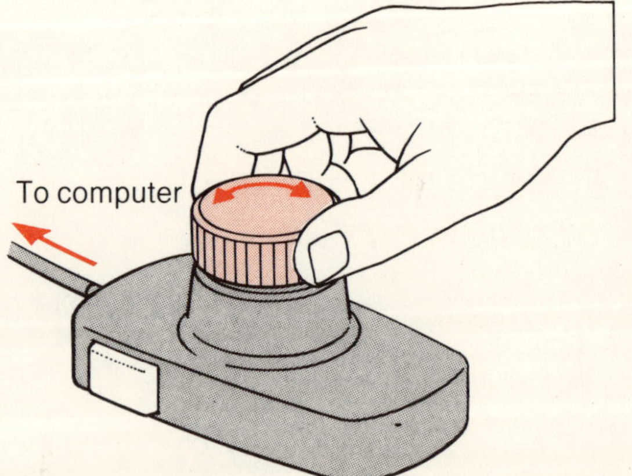

Page
(1) A screen of data on a **VDU** or monitor, or in the case of viewdata systems a set of **frame**s.
(2) Sometimes used to describe the **immediate access store** within a computer, where page zero is all those **location**s whose addresses start with 0, page one addresses start with 1, and so on throughout the available memory.

PAL
Phase **A**lternation **L**ine. System adopted by Britain and some Western European countries for transmitting and receiving colour television signals. See also **NTSC**, **SECAM**.

Palette
The range of colours available for a **graphical display**. Can vary between computers according to the tasks for which each model is designed.

Paper tape
A form of **backing store** that can be read from and written to by the computer. About 2.5 centimetres (1 inch) wide, it has a coded pattern of holes punched across its width, one row or **frame** per character. The most common pattern plans are five-track (up to five holes across), seven-track and eight-track. The sprocket holes that fit on to drive wheel pegs are off centre to prevent the tape being loaded upside down.

Tracks
8 7 6 5 4 3 2 1 Character
0
1
2
3
4
5
6
7
8
9

8 7 6 5 4 3 2 1 Character
@
A
B
C
D
E
F
G
H
I
J
K

Parallel interface

For instance, in an **eight-bit** computer the eight parallel wires or paths along which eight bits of **data** can be sent all at once. This method is much faster than sending items of data one after another as with a **serial interface**. Other machines might use more wires, to match the bigger **word** size.

Parameter

A value passed to or from a **procedure** or **subroutine** during a program run. For example, in a program with a procedure for calculating the floor area of a room (length×breadth) the two measurements of each room would be introduced to the calculations as parameters each time the procedure was used.

Parity bit

An extra **bit** added to each item of data being transmitted so as to make the total number of binary 1s in it always odd (odd parity) or always even (even parity). The receiving computer or **peripheral** can check, and refuse any data item with the wrong parity, asking for it to be sent again. This is a quick and easy way of catching most transmission errors.

Pascal

A **high level language** designed in the early 1970s for writing general programs, which encourages **structured programming**. Named after Blaise Pascal (1623–62), a French mathematician and philosopher who designed a mechanical calculator that could add and subtract.

Password

A secret word or set of characters that allows access to a computer system. Only users who enter the correct version are able to use the system. Used for privacy, security and to prevent unauthorized users from calling up certain programs or using a computer terminal.

PCB

Printed **C**ircuit **B**oard. An electronic **circuit** pattern (usually copper) formed on a thin board of insulating material by an etching process. **Integrated circuits** and other components are then added to complete the circuit. Double-sided boards have a different printed pattern each side connected in places by links passing through the board.

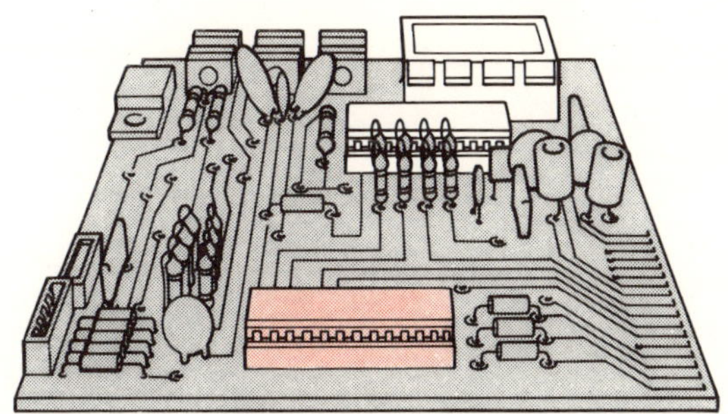

PEEK

A command that causes the content of a particular **memory address** to be displayed on the screen. Used on some computers to increase the speed of a **high level language** program by allowing the user to examine and change a stored value in a manner similar to **machine code**. See also **POKE**.

Peripheral

An item of equipment that can be connected to, and controlled by, a computer but is not part of it. Usually an input, output or storage device, e.g., **bit pad**, **disk drive**, **cassette recorder**, **printer**, **VDU**. Also known as an add-on.

Personal computer

A microcomputer that can, by storing and running its own programs, perform a large amount of the computing requirements of one person without drawing on the power of a larger computer, although it may sometimes access its **database**.

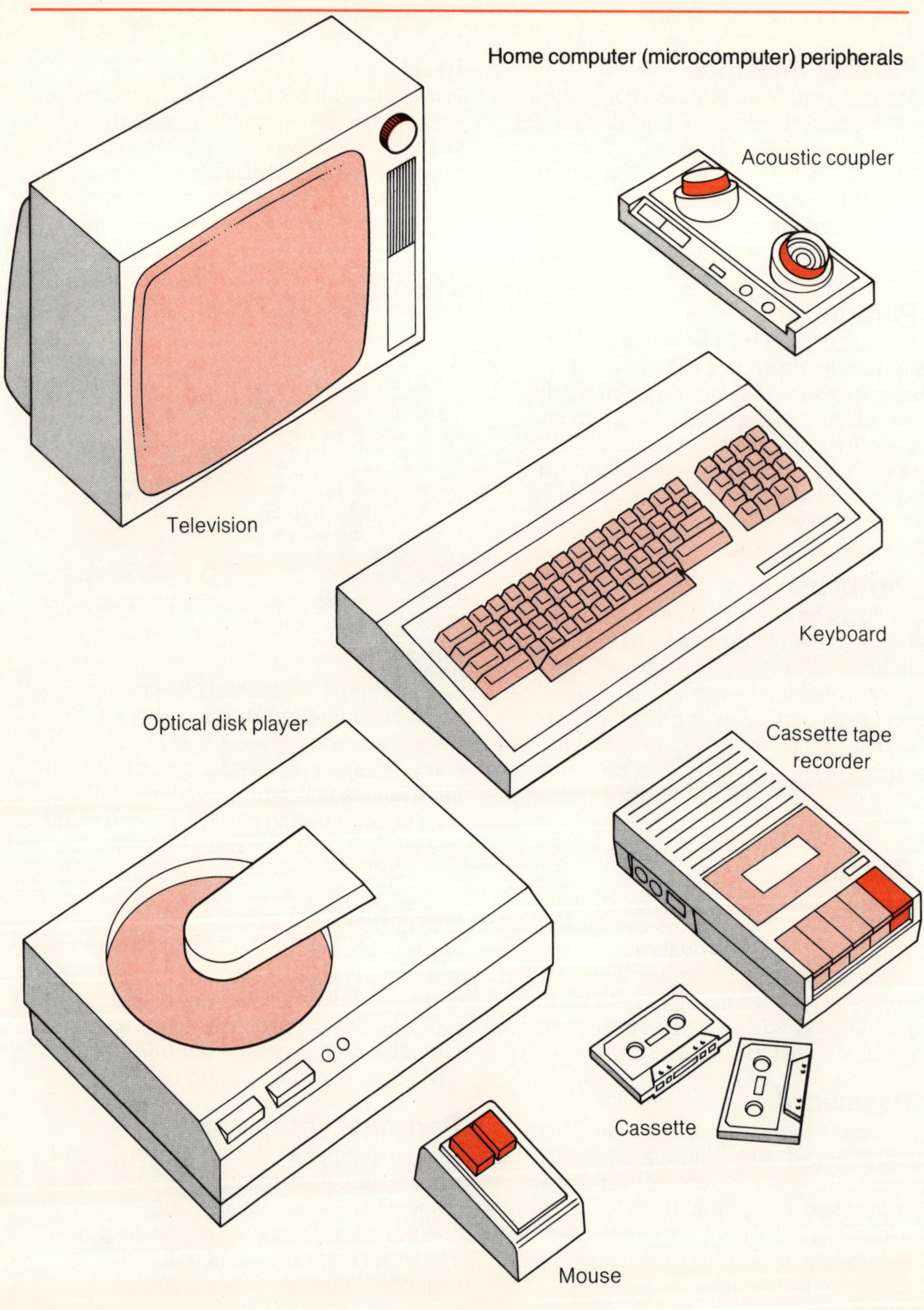
Home computer (microcomputer) peripherals
Acoustic coupler
Television
Keyboard
Optical disk player
Cassette tape recorder
Cassette
Mouse

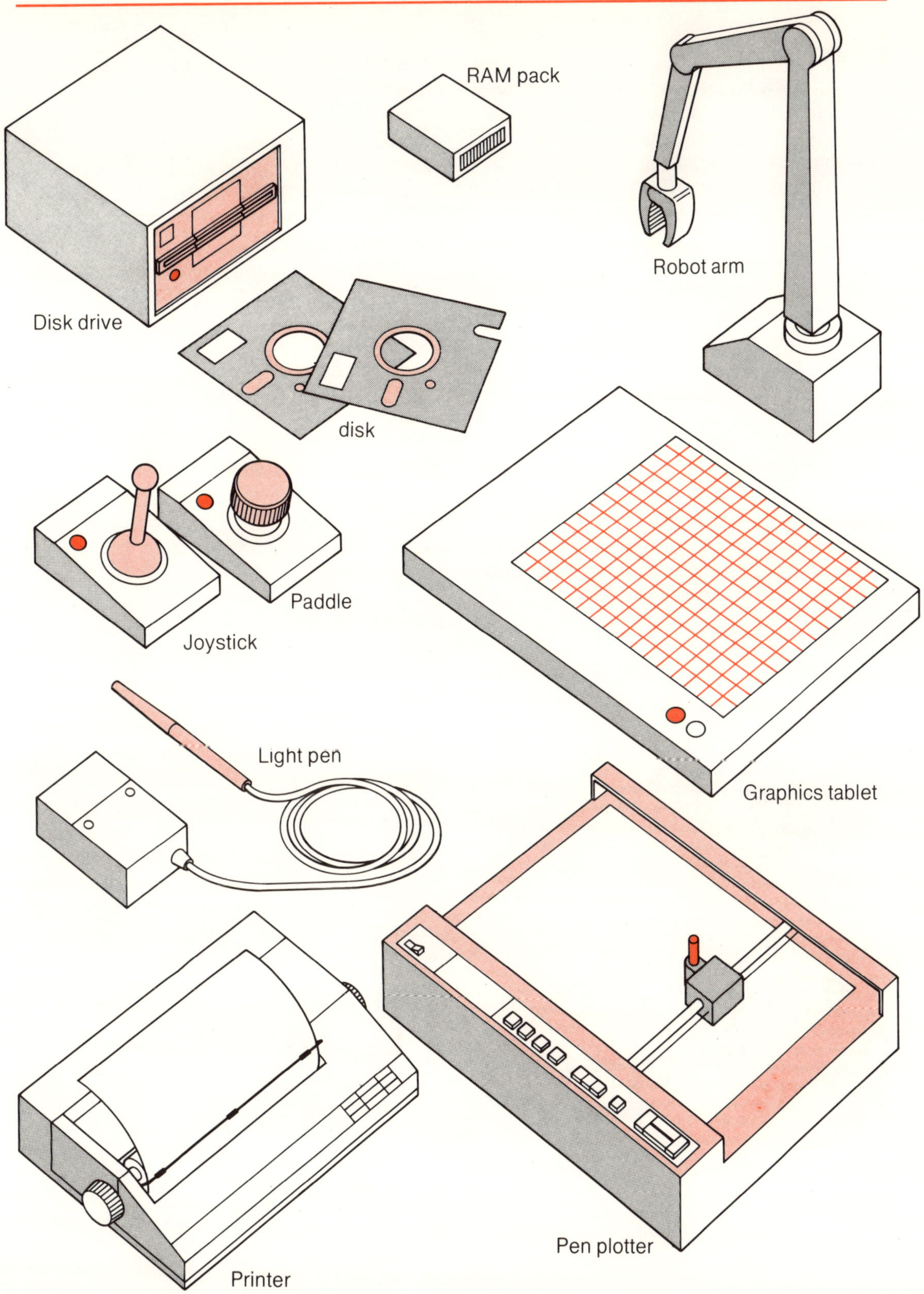
RAM pack
Robot arm
Disk drive
disk
Paddle
Joystick
Light pen
Graphics tablet
Pen plotter
Printer

PILOT
A **programming language** with 14 simple commands that allow the creation of 'question sets' for computer assisted learning (**CAL**) packages. The student is given the next question when the answer is correct but is routed to a 'Help' **frame** if wrong.

Pinfeed
The way that **continuous stationery** is fed into a printer by the teeth or pins of two wheels slotting into the sprocket holes on either side of the paper.

Pixel
Short for '**pic**ture **el**ement', the tiny square many of which together make up all **graphical display**s on a screen. Each pixel's colour and brightness is controlled by the computer, **high resolution graphics** having smaller pixels than graphics shown in low resolution.

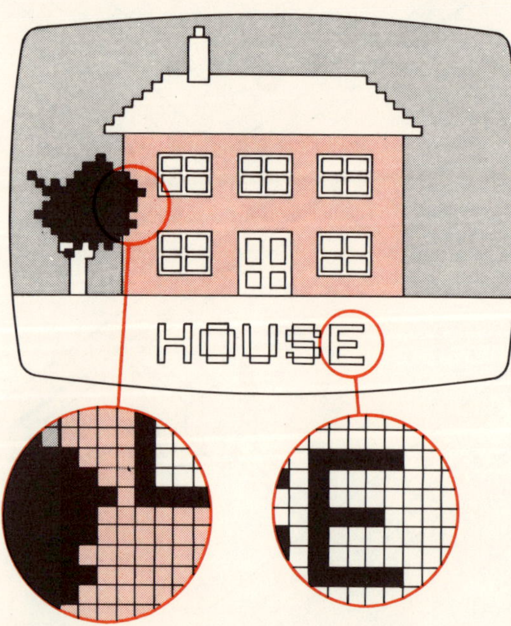

Platen
The part of any printing device against which the paper is pressed while it is being printed (like the 'roller' on a typewriter).

Plato
A very clever and powerful computer based learning (**CBL**) system that took many years to develop. Accessed by special **terminal**s and telegraph lines it is now available in many countries. There is also a microcomputer version.

Plotter
An output device that draws lines on paper under computer control. See **flat-bed plotter**.

Pocket computer
A pocket-size computer, usually battery-powered, with limited memory but capable of storing and running its own programs.

Point-of-sale
Where payment is made for goods bought. The amounts are totalled on an electronic cash register, which will also record other relevant **data**. This could come from a **bar code** reader, an **optical mark reader**, or be keyed in by the operator. The data might include, as well as details of the purchase and its catalogue number, the time of day and the sales assistant's name. In this way a store can keep a check on its stock, monitor its sales performance and note the busy periods so that it can plan more effectively for the future.

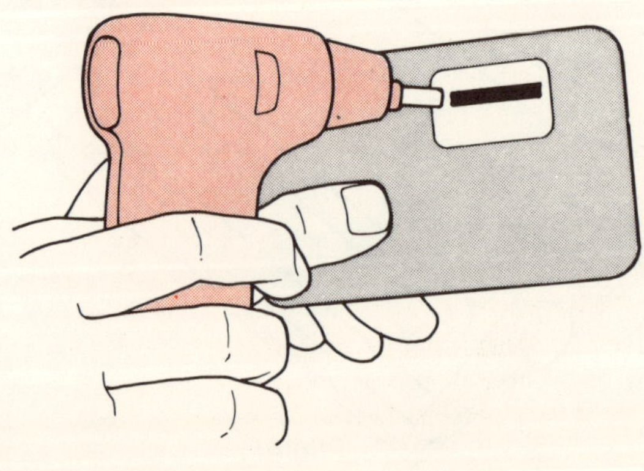

POKE
A command that puts a value into an **address** in the computer's memory. Used with **PEEK** it allows the user to choose which part of the memory will be used to store things, instead of leaving the decision to the computer's own operating system. Being half-way between **BASIC** and **machine code** it increases program speed.

Port
A point at which signals enter or leave the computer. Sometimes a simple socket but could also have an **interface**. Often called an I/O (Input/Output) port.

Prestel
British Telecom's **viewdata** service. Sends signals from one of its central computers to a television set using telephone lines. Information Providers (IPs) rent **pages** to display their goods or services such as motor cars, giftware and package holidays or flight information. Also has 'Gateway' to link to other systems and Closed User Groups (CUGs) where only authorized persons can access the part of memory reserved for that group. Some pages offer computer software. A special television is needed to decode the signals.

Printed circuit board
See **PCB**.

Printer
An output device that, under computer control, produces characters from the **character set** and **graphics character set** on paper. For types of printer and methods used see separate entries: **daisywheel**, **dot-matrix**, **ink-jet**, **laser**, **line**, **thermal**, **thimble** and **xerographic**.

Print head
The part of a printer that forms and prints the **character** shapes onto paper. Being the part most likely to wear out, its 'life' is often measured in 'millions of characters'.

Printout
What a printer produces under computer control. It may consist of hundreds of pages or just half a page.

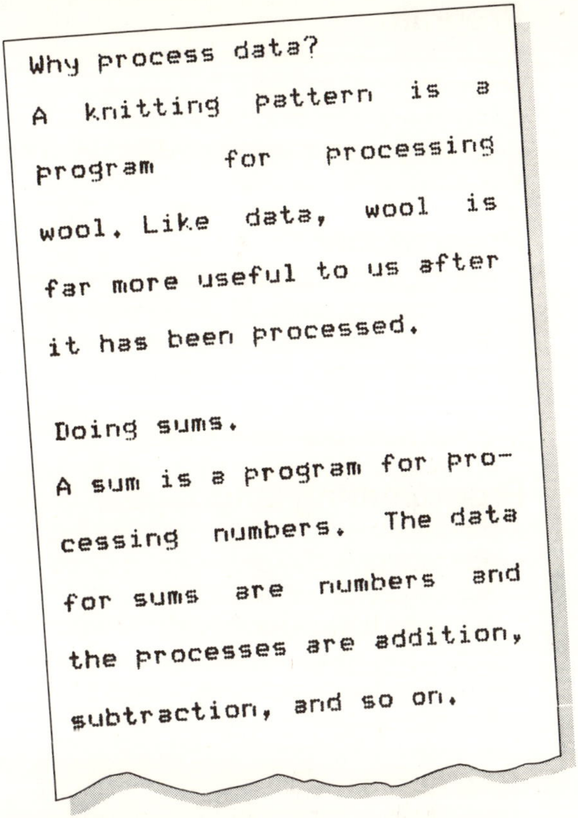

Problem solving
The designing of an **algorithm** from which a computer **program** can be written that will work correctly on any data it is given.

Procedure
(1) A **program** or **routine** designed to do a definite task, that may be 'called' by name from different parts of the main program whenever required. The name indicates what it does and is given to it by the programmer. More useful than a **subroutine**, which is 'called' by its **address**, since it can easily be used by different programs.
(2) The correct way, or series of steps needed, to do something.

Processor
Any **circuit** that can carry out operations on data. The term 'the processor' is generally taken to mean the **central processing unit**.

Program
A complete set of **instructions**, written in a **programming language**, that tell a computer how to do a certain task, step by step. The program works on **data**. See also **algorithm**.

Programmer
A person who writes **programs**, often to a specification prepared by someone else who knows the detail of what is required. After studying this, the programmer can write and test the program to make certain it works in the desired manner.

Programming language
A precise language in which every word used must have only one meaning, and which can be converted into exact instructions the computer will understand. Like people, computers differ in the way they understand things. Just as we often use a different set of words for different jobs, so each computer language is designed to suit a certain range of tasks, and to **run** on a certain family of computers. A program may be in a **high level language** or **low level language**. For different programming languages see separate entries: **assembly language**, **machine code**, **ALGOL**, **BASIC**, **COBOL**, **FORTRAN**, **LOGO**, **Pascal** and **PROLOG**.

PROLOG
From **LOG**ic **PRO**gramming, a **high level language** created in the early 1970s. Can be applied to most computer problems but is a good language for **expert systems** and **fifth generation computers**.

Prompt
A message from the computer telling the user that some action is needed before it can continue. It might consist of words or a flashing symbol on the screen, or just be a light on the keyboard.

Proportional spacing
Printing each **character** with a varying amount of space according to its width. For example, the letters i and l would have less space than m and w. Although a printer must be able to do this, the way the letters are spaced is controlled by the computer's **software**.

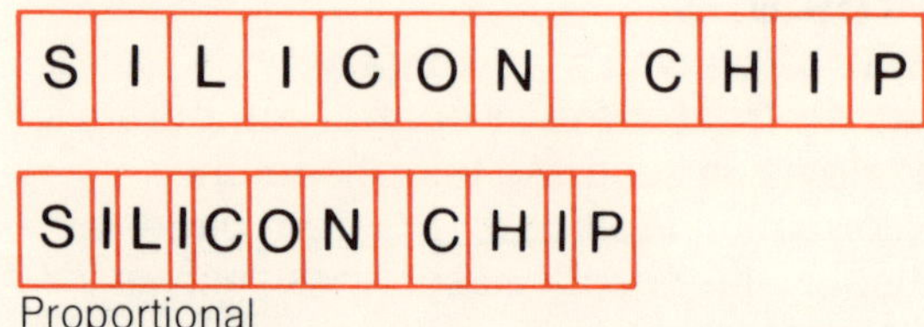

Protocol
A set of rules, found to give the most efficient and error-free running, which decides the order of importance of events in a computer **system**.

Punched card
A card that stores **data** in coded form as a pattern of holes, punched in various positions. The holes can be sensed by a **card reader** and the data passed to a computer. The most common type is the 80-column card, with each column having 12 punching positions. One hole in the 0 to 9 positions are for **digits**, and two or more holes in a column represent alphabetic characters or symbols. See also **card punch**.

Punched tape
See **paper tape**.

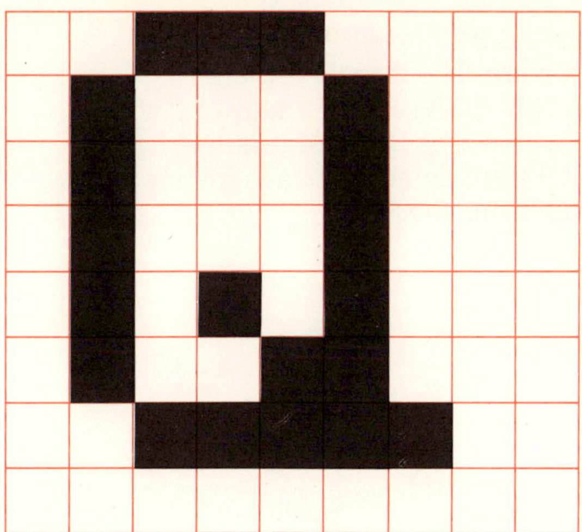

Queue

A list, or a line of data, where new items are added at one end as items are taken from the other end.

QWERTY keyboard

Keyboard found on a standard typewriter. It gets its name from the six letters at the top left of the keyboard. Most computer keyboards are also of this type.

Radix
Latin for 'root'. Any number that is the root, or base, of some number system. For example: 10 is the radix of our **decimal** system; and 2 is the radix of the binary system (see **binary code**). Others would be 8, **octal** and 16, **hexadecimal**.

Random access memory (RAM)
Any memory that allows part of it chosen at random to be read or written to without having to work through from the beginning until the required data is found. Inside a computer, RAM is part of the main memory, and holds the data and programs currently in use. This RAM is **volatile**; other forms of RAM, such as **disk**s, are not. See also **read only memory**.

Random numbers
Numbers produced entirely by chance, but usually within limits set by the user. Most computers have difficulty in working by chance, and give a 'pseudo-random' set of numbers (not truly random) that is sufficient for most purposes.

Raster scan
The series of lines made by the electron beam of a **cathode ray tube** as it sweeps across the screen and builds up the picture. The three international systems, **NTSC** (USA), **PAL** (Britain and most of Europe) and **SECAM** (France) have a different number of lines scanned at different speeds.

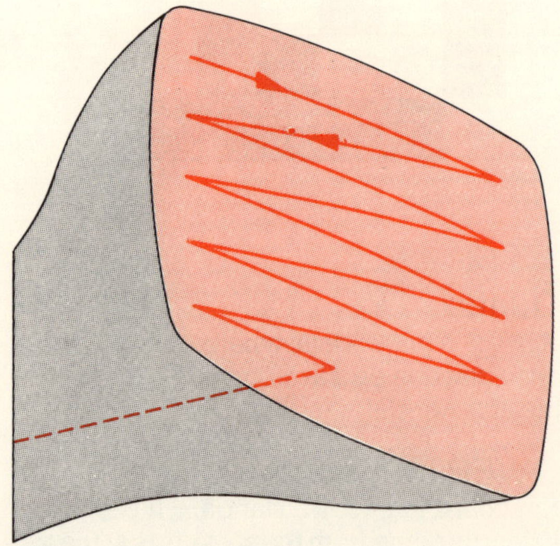

Read only memory (ROM)
Memory that holds **data** or **instructions** fixed permanently at the time of manufacture, and cannot be altered by the computer or programmer. A ROM chip is normally part of a microcomputer's main memory. Examples of ROM include a BASIC (or other language) chip; the **operating system** chip; a **video disk**. See also **EPROM**.

Read/Write head
An electromagnet that reads from or writes to a magnetic storage medium such as **cassette tape** or **disk**. A **disk drive** may have one or more for each disk.

Real time
Describes a **system** that accepts data as an event (such as pressing a button) is happening, processes the data immediately and sends back the results

straight away. For example, pressing the fire button on a joystick to fire a rocket at a Space Invader.

Record files
A systematic way of storing data to be accessed by a computer. To guard against accidents it is important that 'back-up' copies are made. If a file then is changed or updated the earlier copies are kept as back-up. See also **files**.

Refresh
The sending of an electrical pulse through the memory **circuit** at frequent intervals to prevent changes and loss of data. Memory that needs to be refreshed in this way is called 'dynamic'.

Register
A part of the computer's **memory** reserved for a special task or function. A computer may have several registers, including an **accumulator**, and a sequence control register that holds the address of the next **instruction** to be carried out.

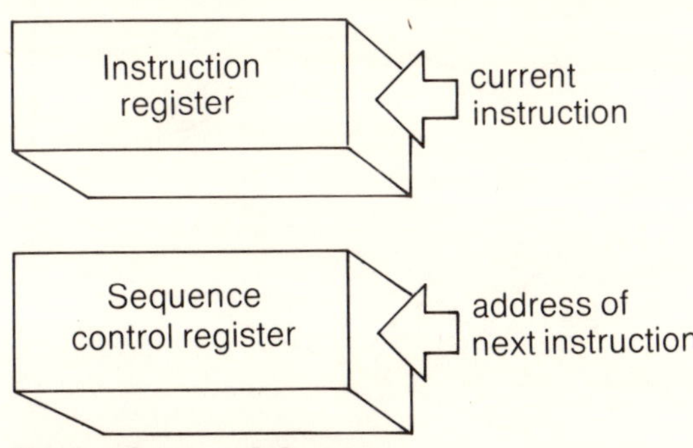

Relative address
A location in memory used by programmers to say where data is stored in relation to a 'base' or bottom-line address; like saying 'Jim lives three doors down from Tom, and Mary lives four doors up from Tom', and so on. When we know Tom's address – the 'base' address – then we can find Jim's and Mary's.

Remote control
Operating from a distance things such as television sets, lights and video recorders, usually by means of a hand-held keypad. This transmits different invisible infra-red signals which act as inputs to the device being controlled. The method enables computers and electronic circuits to be used at a distance for carrying out usually complicated or dangerous tasks. See **robotics**.

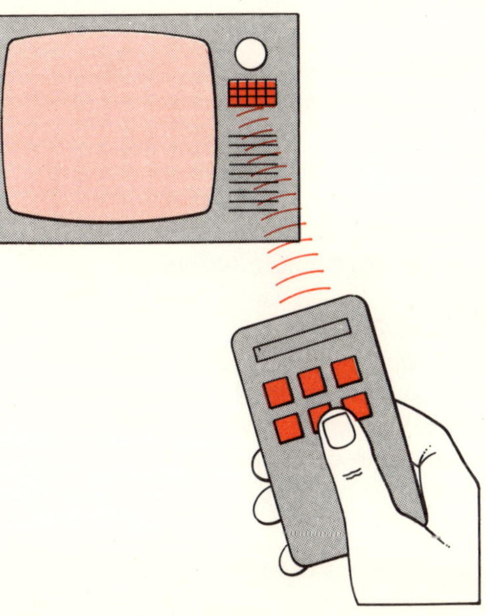

Re-run
To **run** the computer program again from the beginning, using the same data.

Reset
To set a **counter**, or counters, back to zero using a program **instruction**; *or* clear the computer's memory and start again by using a RESET button or **BREAK key**.

Resolution
(1) The quality of a **graphics display**. See **high resolution** and **low resolution graphics**.
(2) The size of step that is to be considered when changing an **analogue** signal to a digital one.

Response time

The time interval between the sending of a signal and the action resulting from that signal being received. For example, the time between pressing a key on the computer keyboard and seeing the result on a screen (almost instantaneous); or the time between dialling a telephone number and hearing the ringing tone (can be several seconds).

RGB output

The computer output which is fed to an RGB **monitor**. Has separate signals for the red, green and blue (RGB) guns of the **cathode ray tube**. These three primary colours make up the **display** or picture. Normally produces pictures of superior quality compared to the output fed to the aerial socket of a colour television.

Ribbon cable

An electrical connection consisting of many, different coloured insulated wires in a flat flexible casing, giving a ribbon-like appearance. Used for **I/O port** connectors that may need up to 40 or even 120 wires.

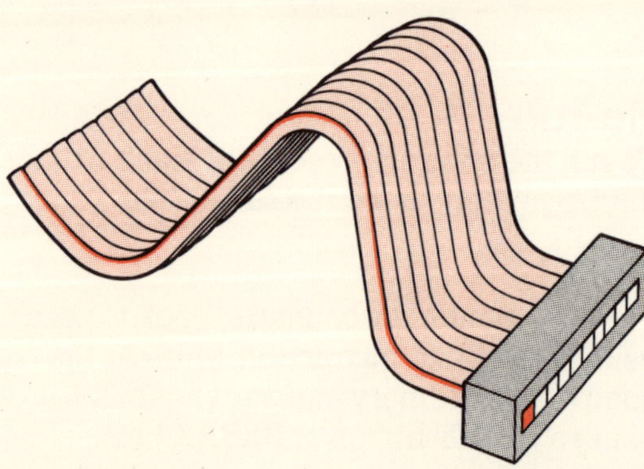

Robotics

The control of a mechanical device such as a robot arm or a satellite tracking aerial dish by a computer or **microprocessor**. The device can usually be programmed to operate 'intelligently', making decisions and learning from mistakes. The connection between computer and device may be made using wires and an **I/O port** or by **remote control**. Sometimes the controlling circuitry is inside the device.

Rogue value

A value, or number, that is completely outside the range of those being input to a running **program**, and used to show that there are no more numbers to come. For example: 9999 could be used as a rogue value when entering the ages of a group of people, but not when entering distances between places. Here a minus value may be used, say −99.

ROM cartridge

Read only memory unit that can be inserted into a suitable socket of a computer and then becomes part of it until it is removed or replaced with another one. Very useful for loading games, business or **utility programs** quickly.

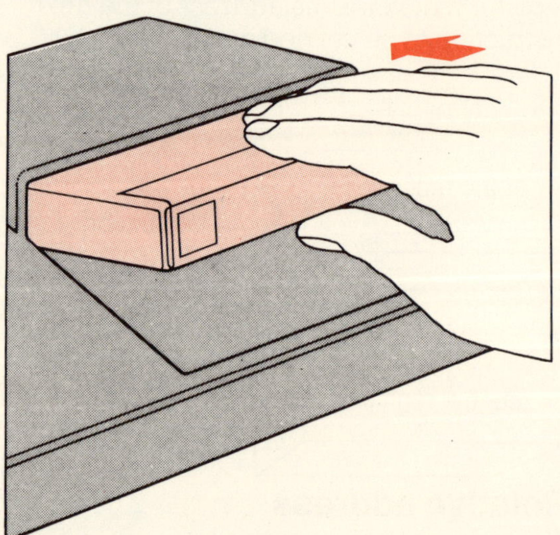

ROM/RAM chips

Read only memory and **random access memory** chips that are within a device and considered part of it, though extra chips can sometimes be added. Compare **ROM cartridge**.

Rounding

A method of reducing the total **digit**s in a number while keeping its accuracy within set limits. For decimal numbers the rule is usually: 5 and above go one higher, below 5 go one lower. For example:

Rounding	16.36582
to four decimal places becomes	16.3658
to three places,	16.366
to two places, (say, for money)	16.37

Compare **truncation**.

Routine

Something that is the same every time. A computer is very good at doing routine tasks. A routine is written as a self-contained **program** with a definite job to do and may form a part of many different programs. For example, a general purpose **input** routine.

RS232 interface

The most common **serial interface**. It usually connects via a 25-way plug. The V24 port can be assumed to be identical for all purposes; the RS423 is another similar interface.

Run

(1) To make a computer execute (carry out) a **program**.
(2) A **command** understood by some computers and included in some programming languages, meaning 'Execute the program'.

S100 Bus
A system of electrical connections used to transfer data inside a microcomputer between various **circuit** boards and the **motherboard**. Has up to 100 lines: 16 for the **address bus**, 16 for the **data bus**, 35 for the control bus and the rest for power supplies.

SAVE
A **command** understood by most microcomputers to mean 'Store on a **cassette tape** or **disk** the program that is now in the computer's memory'. Generally, the program is given a name, say 'Diary', so the command becomes SAVE 'Diary'.

Scan
(1) To examine and test every item in a list or **file** to see if it meets certain conditions.
(2) To test each input/output channel to see if it is in use.
(3) The movement of the electron beam forming the picture on the screen of a cathode ray tube. See **raster scan**.

Scheduling
Organizing jobs for the computer, and putting them in the order in which the computer can do them with maximum efficiency. May be performed by the operator or by the computer. The availability of a printer and other **peripherals** will affect the priority given to any job.

Schema
An outline description, chart or diagram showing the route or method used to access a **file** or **database**.

Scratch pad memory
An area of computer's memory reserved for the carrying out of small calculations, the results of which are held for use as required. Sometimes called a 'working store'.

Screen
The front surface of a **cathode ray tube** or **LCD** upon which can be displayed computer text and graphics. See also **monitor**, **television set** and **VDU**.

Scroll
The movement of the display on a screen, or in a **window**, to allow a large picture to be viewed in sections. Most microcomputers can be set to scroll both vertically and horizontally, continuously, or a line, column or screenful at a time.

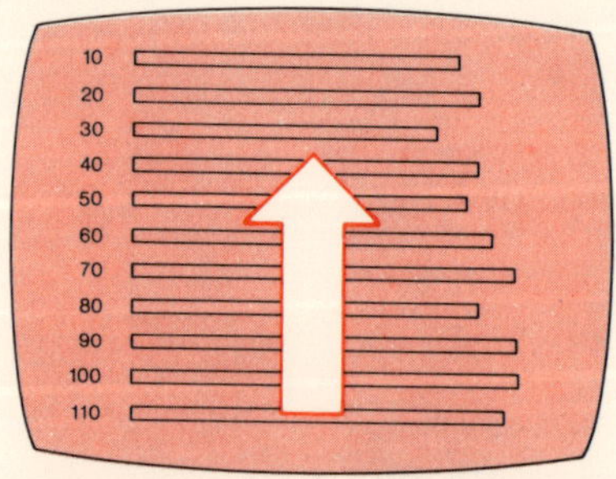

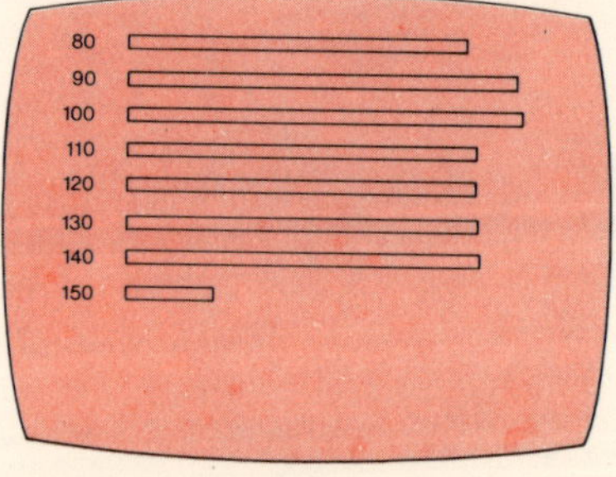

Vertical scroll

SECAM
Système **E**n **C**ouleurs **A** **M**émoire, the French standard for transmitting television pictures. See also **PAL** and **NTSC**.

Second generation computers
Computers such as **Atlas**, built between mid-1950s and mid-1960s, that used **transistor**s in place of **valve**s. This made them much more reliable. They were also smaller and used less power, yet had far greater computing capability.

Sector
A section of a magnetic **disk**, like a slice of cake. The disk's circular tracks are divided by the lines forming the sectors. The computer reads or writes each sector track as a block, with its own **address**. A **minifloppy** is usually divided into 10 sectors, a **hard disk** into 32 sectors. See also **hard sectored** and **soft sectored**.

Semiconductor
A material that is somewhere between a good conductor of electricity and an insulator (a very poor conductor). Can change its conductive powers and the way it conducts when small amounts of another substance are added. The basis of the **transistor** and other **solid state** electronic components. Today, **silicon** is the most widely used semiconductor.

Sequential processing
Taking a set of stored records from the computer's **memory** or **backing store** and dealing with each one in order. To be sequential rather than serial, such records have to be sorted or grouped into a logical order before being processed.

Serial interface
Interface that transmits each **bit** of a block of data in order, one after another, along a wire or cable, although the interface may have many wires for a variety of applications. The Electrical Industries Association's standard **RS232 interface** is one example. See also **parallel interface**.

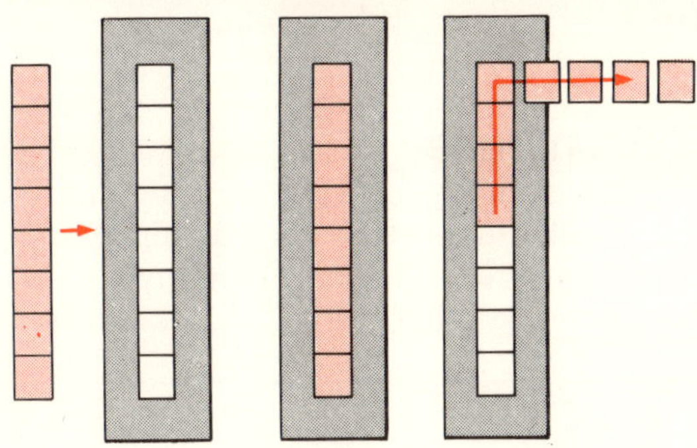

SHIFT and SHIFT LOCK keys
On a computer keyboard, keys that give a 'second function' action to most keys, changing **lower case** letters to **upper case** and numbers to other various symbols. **ASCII code** is designed to utilize this system.

Shift register
A **location** within the central processing unit which allows the **bits** held to be moved left or right as instructed. In binary arithmetic a shift left will double the value (one, two, four, eight etc.), and a shift right will halve it (one, a half, a quarter, one eighth etc.). With decimals, moving one column to the left or right has the effect of multiplying or dividing by 10.

Signal
An electrical pulse, produced by variations in the voltage, used to pass **data** through an electronic circuit or system. Computers use on/off, high/low or +/− voltage to indicate 1 or 0 in **binary code**.

Silicon chip
An **integrated circuit** on a wafer of silicon a few millimetres square. Can be a **microprocessor**, **memory** or other circuit.

Silicon disk
An assembly of **RAM chips** inside the computer that can be accessed like a **floppy disk**. Offers much faster **access times** but its contents have to be copied at the end of use as it is a 'volatile' memory (it loses the data when the machine is switched off).

Silicon Valley
The region of California in the USA where the development of the **silicon chip** was carried out. Now the home of many computer manufacturers.

Simulation
To make a model of a system that will respond to the decisions and actions of the user and give results similar to those in a 'real life' situation. Very useful for training in situations where real-life errors may be dangerous and costly. Also allows 'what if...' questions to be studied. See **flight simulator**.

Single density
Describes a way of packing data on a **disk**. Term used to distinguish from **double density**, after improvements in manufacture enabled more data to be packed into each track.

Soft sectored
Type of **disk** that needs **software** to mark, with magnetic signals, the sections or **sectors** of recording tracks. See also **hard sectored.**

Software
The collection of computer **programs** and service **routines** needed to make the computer and other **hardware** work. See also **library software**.

Solid state
Describes any electronic device made of solid material and without moving parts, which depends only on the behaviour of electrons for its functioning. See **semiconductor**.

Sort
To arrange **data** items in a particular order so as to allow fast and efficient processing of the data. The order could be alphabetical, numerical, or by size, colour or location – whichever is the most suitable. See also **bubble sort**.

Sound synthesizer
Inside some computers, special electronic circuit for producing sound. The sound can then be heard in the normal way through a television set or through a separate loudspeaker. See also **channel**, **envelope**.

Source language
The language used by a **programmer** to write a source program that will be translated by the computer into an **object program**; a source language cannot be directly understood by the computer. See also **high level language**.

Speech recognition

The ability of the computer to interpret the spoken word by comparing it with those held in **memory**. The computer acts as instructed by the **program**. It does not understand what is said, it only recognizes it. For example, the programmer could easily make the computer divide every time it recognizes the word 'add'.

Speech synthesis

The ability of some computers to make sounds similar to human speech on receiving **digital** signals, whether from a keyboard or from data accessed by a program. Can be used to give a one or two word description when an item number is entered.

Spreadsheet program

Program in which data is held on a large 'sheet' in the computer's memory, any part of which can be called up and seen on the screen. The 'sheet' is laid out in columns and rows and the user can enter text, numbers or a formula as required. Any alteration made by the user in one position can result in immediate and appropriate changes in other positions by the computer. Used mostly for financial modelling to help the user to evaluate the results of different actions before taking them, and avoid lengthy calculations by hand.

________	Accounts for 1983, in $		
	Sales	Costs	Profit
January	567	234	233
February	892	298	594
March	549	346	203
April	653	402	251
May	874	108	766
June	358	235	123
July	984	420	544
August	874	305	569
September	386	143	243
October	487	203	284
November	765	485	280
December	954	364	590

Sprite

Part of the **graphics character set**. Usually a largish shape that can be designed by the user, called from the computer's memory and moved around the screen as a whole. See also **user defined graphics**.

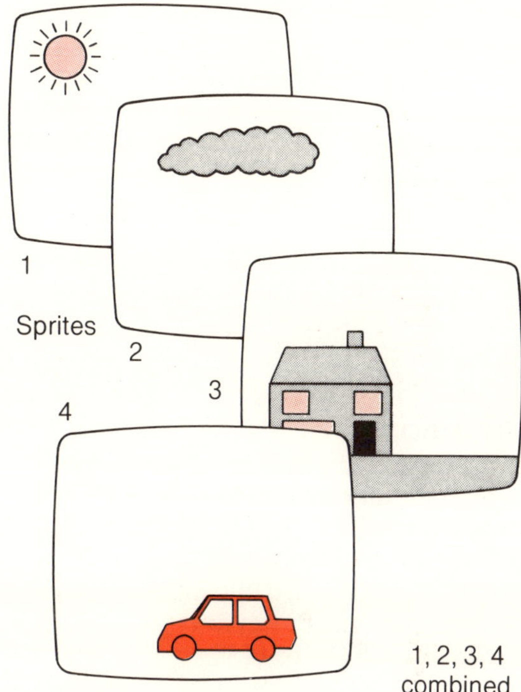

Sprites

1, 2, 3, 4 combined

Sprocket holes
A series of holes in **paper tape** and along the edges of **continuous stationery** to enable them to be driven by sprocket wheels through a printer or other device at a regulated speed or in measured steps.

Stack
An area of the computer's **memory** used to hold temporary data on a 'last in, first out' basis. As an item is added or removed from the end, previously stored items move one place as if stacked on top of each other.

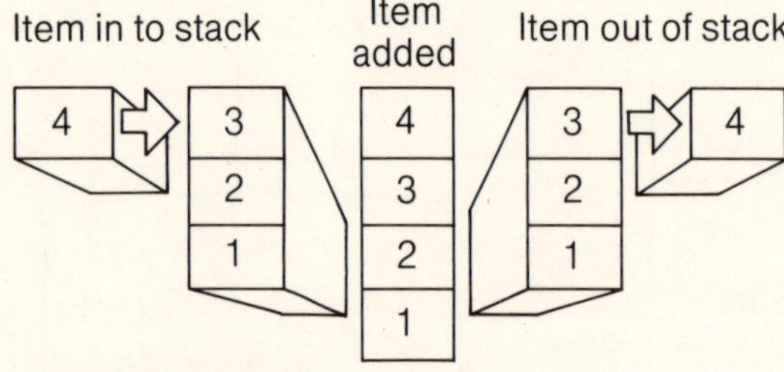

Statement
An **instruction** in a **high level language**. When translated by a **compiler** or **interpreter** will result in several **machine code** instructions. In BASIC each statement starts with a line number and is followed by a BASIC keyword, e.g. 100 PRINT, 25 GOTO, 150 LIST.

Store
(1) Any **memory** of a computer system that holds **data** or **programs**.
(2) To put data into a memory.
See also **backing store**.

String
A list of **characters** stored by a computer as data. For example, 'Address string' may hold data representing '36 High Street', and be held in an area of memory reserved for storing strings, each with its own computer **address**. Note that a number in string form (e.g. 36, as above) would have to be changed to numeric form before being used in mathematical calculations.

Stringy floppy
A storage device that uses magnetic tape in a continuous loop. Allows faster **access time** than a normal cassette tape and uses cheaper drive units than **disks**. Also known as floppy tape.

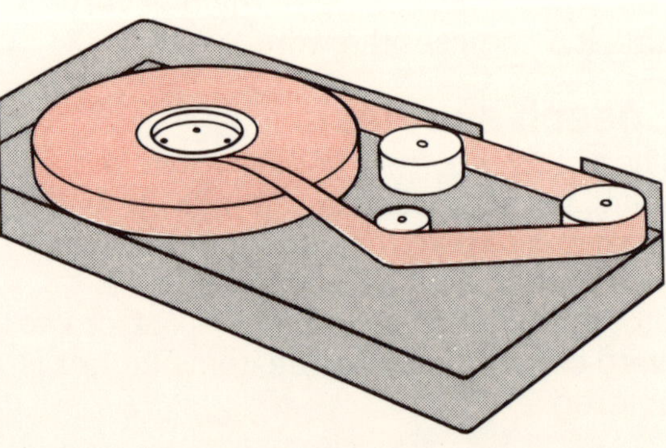

Structured programming
A way of designing a **program** that divides it into a series of sections (modules) or **procedures**, each doing a clearly defined task that is a logical part of the original and can be tested independently. With good documentation such programs can be amended or updated with little risk of **bugs**, as each alteration can only affect one section. See also **top down approach**.

Subroutine
A small section of a **program** that does a certain task, with a definite **address** or line number that the main program can branch to as often as required. The last instruction in a subroutine is usually 'Return to main program'. For example:
1000 (description of subroutine)
1010 (statements making up subroutine)
1200 RETURN

Subscript
(1) Character, usually a digit, added to a **variable** to distinguish it from others, e.g. A1, A2, A3, . . .; or to identify an item in a **one-** or **two-dimensional array**, e.g. STUDENT (3A,7).

(2) Digit or other character written small, after a number, and below the line to indicate its **radix**.

10100_2 is in **binary code**.

32_6 is in base 6.

24_8 is in **octal**.

20_{10} is in decimal.

14_x is in **hexadecimal**.

(3) A facility found on some **printer**s that enables smaller characters to be printed just below the line, e.g. in chemical formulae, H_2O, O_2, H_2SO_4.

Superscript

A facility found on some **printer**s that enables smaller characters to be printed just above the line, e.g. as used when expressing powers: 9^2 (9 to the power of 2) =81.

Synchronous mode

Describes when all the computer's operations are controlled by equally spaced **clock** pulses, usually generated by an **oscillator**.

Syntax

The **language** rules that any programmer must follow to ensure that each **instruction** is written exactly as required by the **assembler**, **compiler** or computer.

System

Basically, everything needed to perform a complete job using a computer. This includes all the necessary **hardware**, **software** as well as people to operate the machines.

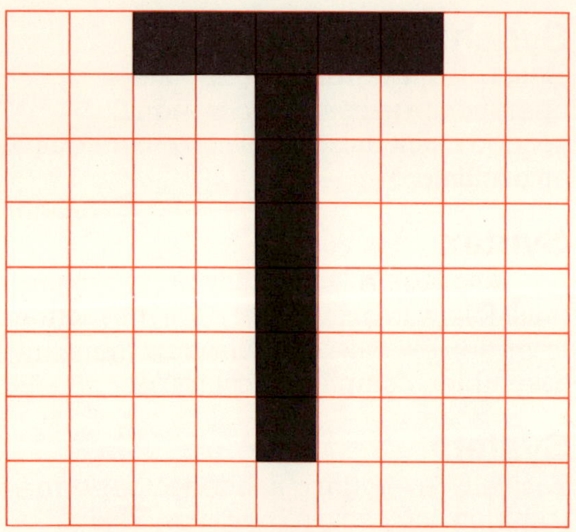

Telesoftware
Software sent from one computer to another by wire, cable, radio waves or satellite transmission. Available with **teletext** and with **viewdata** systems.

Teletext
Pages of text and **low resolution** graphics broadcast using part of the normal television signal. The service offers news, advertising and other information as well as **telesoftware**. A decoder captures and uses the signal to fill the whole screen with the page you select.

Table
An example of a **two-dimensional array** where the data in one column is related to that in other columns.

Tabulator
A machine for adding and analysing the data on **punched cards**, invented by **Hollerith** in the 1890s. The operator had to make correct connections by inserting wires with plugs into holes. Later developed to handle other calculations and **printout**.

Tape recorder
A device that enables data to be stored on **magnetic tape**. Large computer systems use wide tape on reels; microcomputers use narrow tape in cassettes.

Telecoms/Telecommunications
The transfer of information over large distances by wire, cable, radio waves or satellite transmission. Involves television programs, computer data etc.

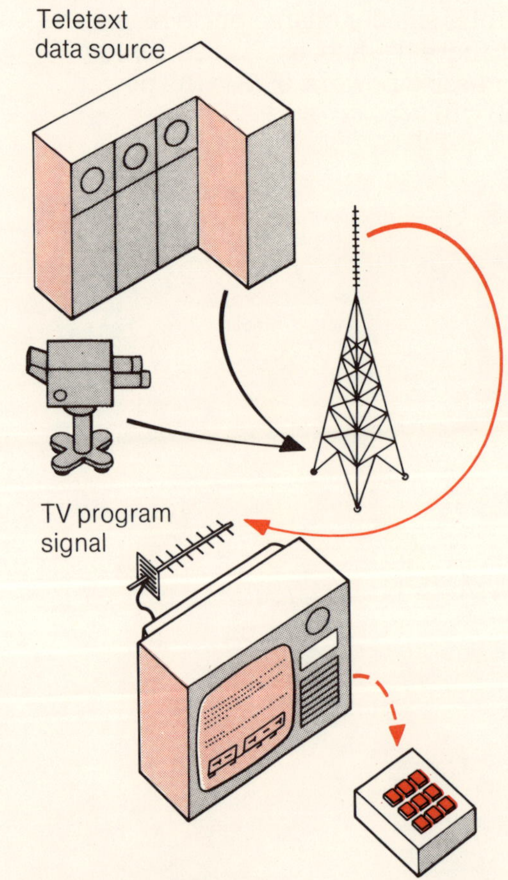

Teleprinter
An input/output device that can send and receive **data** over distances, giving **printout** and/or **punched tape**. Similar to a typewriter in looks and action.

Television set
An item of **hardware** that takes a radio wave signal from an aerial or cable and converts it into a picture on a screen as well

as sound. The major part is a **cathode ray tube**. May also act upon such signals from a video recorder, electronic game or a microcomputer.

Telex
A system that uses **teleprinter**s and the telephone system to provide a world-wide automatic data and information exchange service for subscribers. Much used in offices.

Terminal
Any device allowing **input** and **output** of data used with a computer system that is usually some distance away.

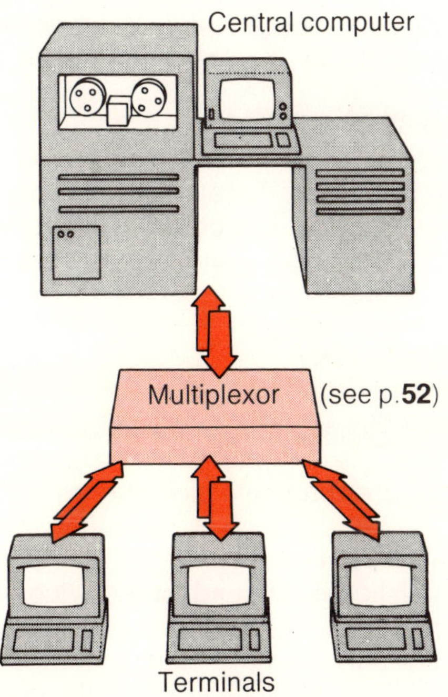

Terminator
A **signal**, mark or **rogue value** used to indicate the end of a stream of data.

Test data
Data used to try out a **program**, **procedure** or **subroutine**, and check the output. Covers as many likely, and unlikely **input**s as is reasonable.

Text
Letters, numbers and words, as distinct from pictures, diagrams and **graphics**. Does not include **header**s, **terminator**s or **control character**s.

Text editor
A **program** that will automatically design or lay out text on a page or screen during writing and while insertions, deletions, and corrections are being made.

Thermal printer
A printer that forms visible **character**s from dots produced by heated wires turning heat-sensitive paper black.

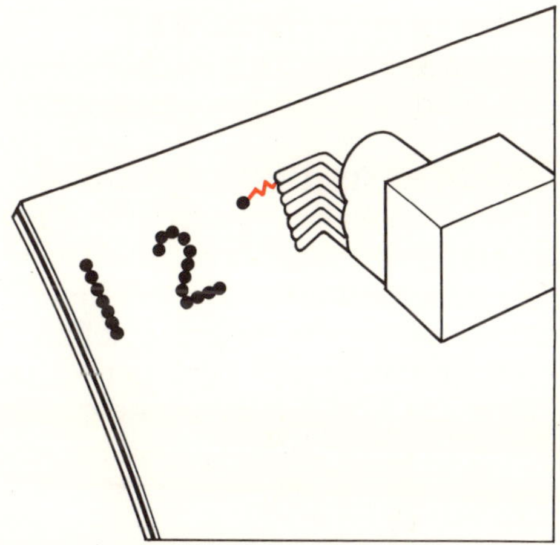

Thimble printer
A printer with a revolving, thimble-shaped **print head**. The characters, which are spaced round its shell, press an inked ribbon onto the paper as data is received from a computer.

Third generation computers
Computers produced between 1966 and 1979 in which **integrated circuit**s replaced the **transistor**s which had been the basic components in the second generation computers. See also **fourth generation computer**s.

Timesharing
A system that allows two or more people, working from **terminal**s and often many kilometres apart, to use the same computer at the same time. Generally, they will not be aware of anyone else using the system because the computer's speed of working reduces waiting time to an unnoticed amount.

Top down approach
A method of solving a problem by breaking it down into small units or **module**s. The first module is worked out and during its design the need for other modules will become clear and these too are then specified. In their design, smaller sub-modules may become necessary and so on. This leads to **structured programming** and each module in turn has to be specified, designed, built and tested.

Touch sensitive keyboard
A keyboard with no moving parts. The pressure of one's finger or just its presence is registered electrically as an **input**. Has the advantage of there being nothing to wear out and no gaps between keys to collect dirt. Can also we wiped clean. Found on many microcomputers, calculators, cash dispensers and television sets.

Trace
A piece of **software** or **firmware** that allows a program to be checked during an actual run to ensure that all the **instruction**s, **procedure**s and **subroutine**s are 'called' in the correct order. The results at each step can be examined and their accuracy checked by displaying them on the screen or by printing them out. Used for the **debugging** of programs.

Tractor feed
A method of smoothly feeding **continuous stationery** through a printer, under computer control, using the sprocket holes along the edges of the paper to drive it through. Often, there are several sprocket wheels each side for guiding the paper before and after it reaches the **platen**.

Transaction file
The record of all the daily, weekly or monthly changes that at a later time need to be transferred to a **record file** or **database**. Avoids having to be **on line** to a computer all the while.

Transducer
Any device that changes electrical energy to energy in another form, or vice-versa. For example, a **digital plotter** converts electrical energy into movement.

Transistor
A small, light **semiconductor** device invented in 1948, which can act as an amplifier and as a two-state, either/or switch. This two-state ability is the basis of both **solid state** memory, in that a 0 or 1 can be stored (see **binary code**), and the **logic gate** switching circuit.

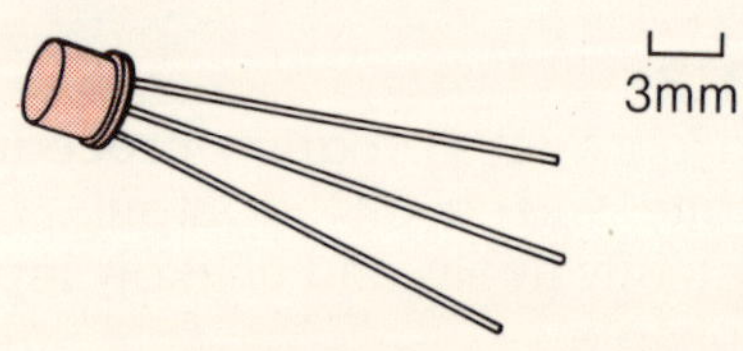

Tree structure

Just as a tree has a trunk which divides into branches that further divide into more branches, so a computer program can be built up in the same way (see **top down approach**). **Data**, too, can be stored in a 'tree' for quicker access by a program.

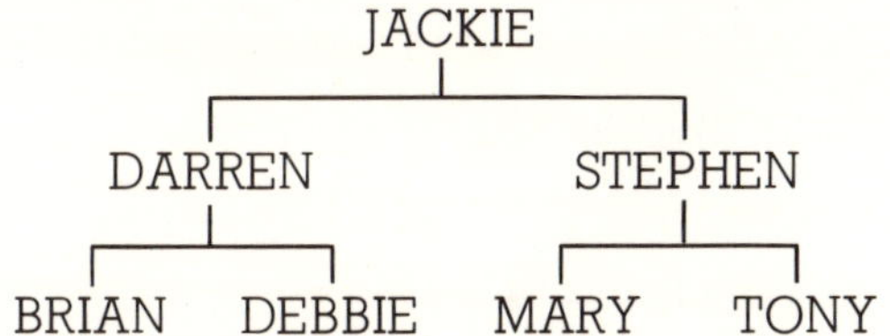

STEPHEN is accessed in two steps using a tree structure (first access the 'root' JACKIE, then the right-hand 'branch') whereas it would require six steps if the names were stored in alphabetical order.

Truncation

In arithmetic, a method of reducing a number to a certain number of significant figures. Unlike **rounding**, it cuts off the remaining figures without regard to their value. For example, truncation to four significant figures results in,
158.72 and 158.79 both becoming 158.7
12,341 and 12,348 both becoming 12,340.

Truth table

A table that shows clearly, using 0s and 1s all the possible outputs of a **logic gate** or **logic circuit** made up of a combination of logic gates. See **AND**, **NOT** and **OR gate**s.

Turnkey

A computer system designed to start working and do a particular job at the turn of a key. The user is guided on how to input data by the computer and the automatically loaded (self-booting) **software**. See also **application package** and **user friendly**.

Turtle

An output device whose movements can be controlled by a computer. The turtle may have wheels and move on the floor, marking lines and avoiding objects (floor turtle), or it may be a light on a **screen** that draws bright coloured lines faster than the eye can follow (light turtle). **LOGO** is generally the computer language used to communicate with a turtle.

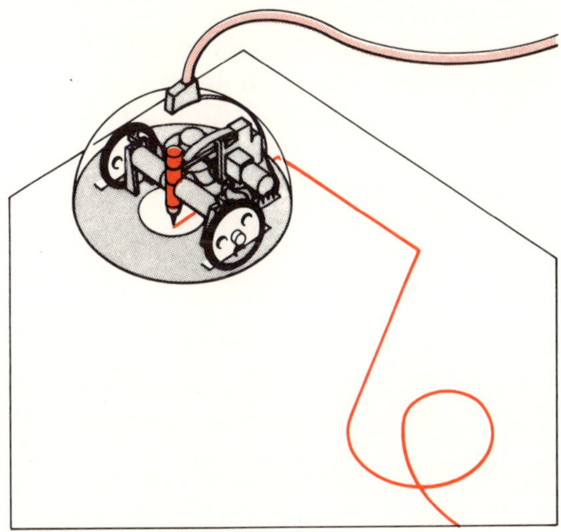

Turtle graphics

Part of an **interactive program**, such as **LOGO**, that allows the user to design, draw, repeat and change a screen picture using a light **turtle**. Commands such as 'forward 80' and 'right 45' are normally used, but the user can also design **procedure**s such as 'square' and 'triangle'.

Two-dimensional array

A way of storing **data** in rows and columns, with each item being identified by two **subscript**s. For example, the computer record of a student who is seventh on the register of class 3A would be identified and accessed in the student **file** by 'STUDENT(3A,7)'. A soccer league table, listing the teams and their results (played, won, drawn etc.) in columns, is a similar type of array. To find out a specific detail about a team – goals scored, for example – you read across the appropriate row and down the respective column.

Two's complement

A method of storing negative numbers, used by many computers. For example, in four-digit **binary code** the decimal number 5 is held as 0101 (=4+1, as the column values are 8, 4, 2, 1). Decimal −5 is held as the two's complement of 0101, that is 1011. This is obtained by taking the **complement** of 0101 and then adding 1. Thus,
0101 becomes 1010 (complement)
1010+1=1011 (two's complement)
Thus −5 is held not as −0101 but as 1011 (= −8+0+2+1).

Typeface

The shape, or style, of the **character**s used by a printer or typewriter to make marks on paper.

1234567890()='%$£!?*+@

1234567890()='%$£!?*+@

1234567890()='%$£!?*+@

1234567890()='%$£!?*+@

1234567890()='%$£!?*+@

1234567890()='%$£!?+@*

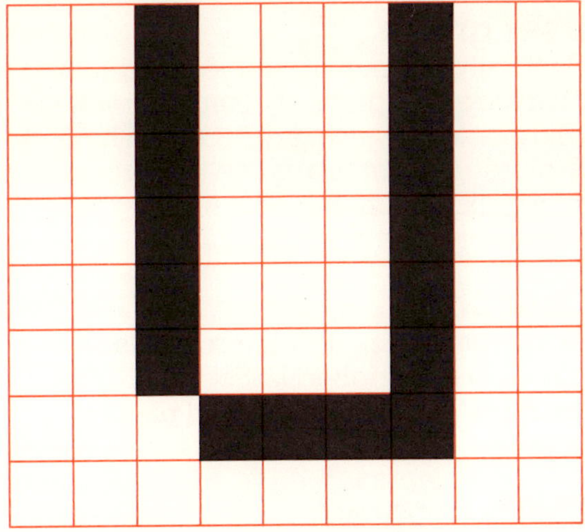

ULA/Uncommitted logic array
An **integrated circuit** having sets of **logic circuit**s that are not connected up to each other. This enables the purchaser to specify the final circuit pattern to meet his or her needs and to get a specially designed chip at a low cost.

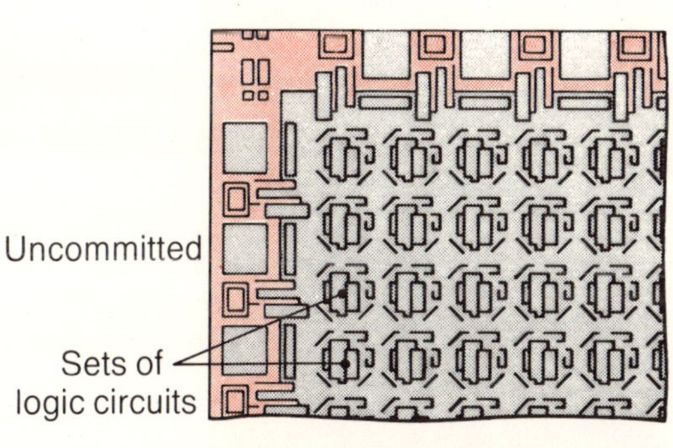

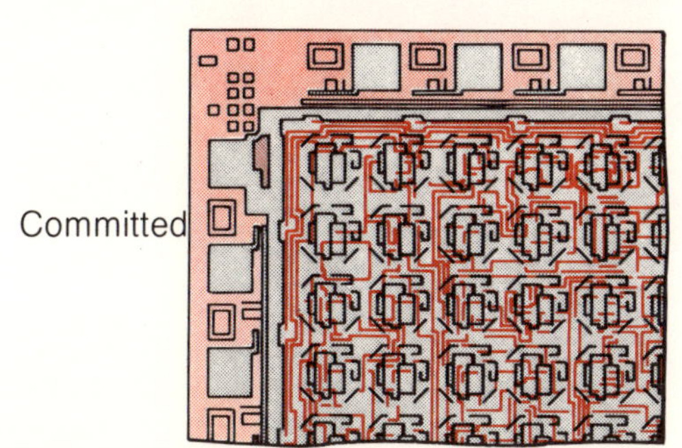

UNIVAC 1
One of the first commercial computers, bought by the United States Census Bureau in 1951 for over $2 million. Today a computer of equivalent power would cost less than $400 and consist of a single printed circuit board (**PCB**). UNIVAC 1 was most notable for the use of **magnetic tape** to input data.

Up and running
Means that a computer system, including **hardware** and **software**, is working satisfactorily. Can also describe a series of programs performing as designed, after **debugging**.

Update
(1) To change a **program** so as to allow for changed circumstances, e.g. changes in income tax law, currency values or exam passmarks.
(2) To change the data held in **record file**s or a **database**. For example, stock and/or sales records could be changed to give up-to-date figures, using a **transaction file**. A residents list would need to be updated to keep track of births, deaths and people moving to or from the locality.

Upgrade
To improve the specification and performance of any **hardware**, **firmware** or **software**. Upgraded hardware will not accept original software if it is not **compatible**.

Upper case letters
Capital letters, as distinct from small, or 'lower case' letters. On a computer keyboard, usually obtained by pressing the SHIFT key along with the chosen letter key.

User
A person operating (with their 'hands on') any part of a computer system. See also **user friendly**.

User defined graphics

Graphics characters created from character codes that have not been fixed by the computer manufacturer and are available to the user. These additional graphics characters can be stored for later use.

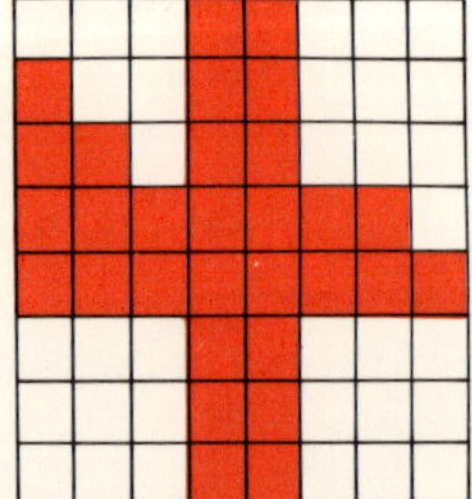

User friendly

Easy to use, leaving the user in no doubt about what the next action or input should be. A user-friendly program can cope with incorrect actions or inputs without going wrong, and provide opportunity for input to be re-entered.

User group

Generally, a group of people using similar **hardware**, **program**s or computer systems, who meet together or are in contact by post. A 'closed user group' is one that provides information for members belonging to a particular trade or profession.

User port

An **interface** socket on the computer for plugging in **peripheral**s. See **centronics interface**, **serial interface**, and **parallel interface**.

Utility program

(1) Part of a larger **program** designed to do a commonplace task such as a **sort** or a transfer of data from one device to another. (2) A 'stand-alone' program designed to assist with the writing or **debugging** of programs or **procedure**s.

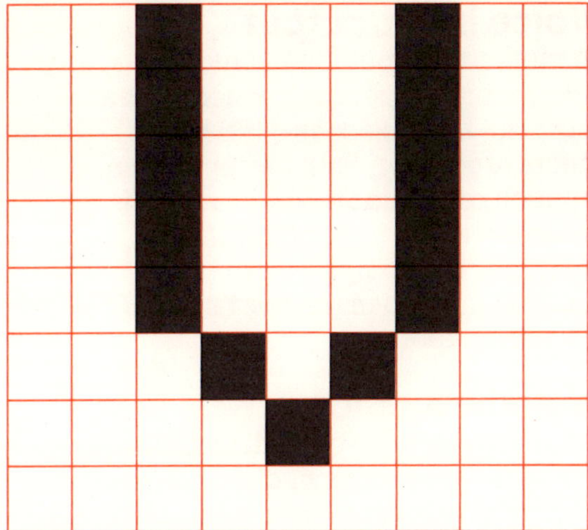

Validity check
A test that ensures that input **data** is reasonable, complete and accurate. For example, a diary **routine** could check that the 'day of the month' did not exceed 31.

Valve
An electrical component used in radios, television sets and computers to control the flow of current and store data before the **transistor** was invented. First generation computers such as **LEO** and **UNIVAC 1** were built with electronic valves.

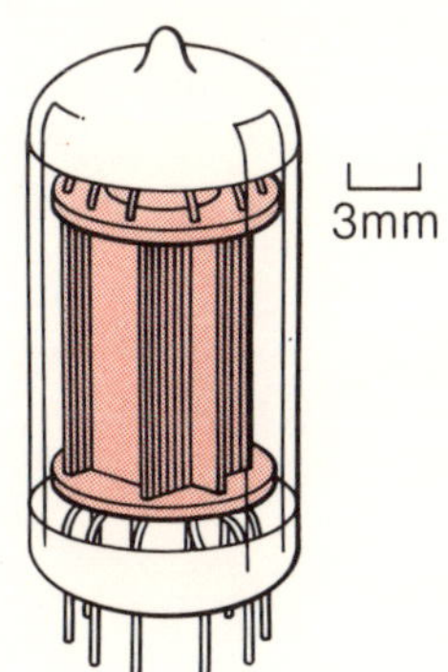

Variable
A character or characters referring to an area of computer memory that can hold numerical values (numerical variable) or a **string** of characters (string variable). Thus, if variable B4 is given the value 18, then the location in memory called B4 will hold 18 until a later **instruction** changes it or the computer is switched off. String variables may require several locations.

VDU/Visual display unit
An output device mainly consisting of a **cathode ray tube** (CRT), on which **text** and **graphics** can be displayed. Sometimes also has a keyboard. See also **monitor** and **television set**.

Verifier
A machine used to check **punched card**s and **paper tape** by comparing them with data being re-typed on its keyboard.

Video disk
A storage device that is read by a video disk player using a laser beam. As with a video tape machine the output is displayed on a television screen. Disks offer faster and more accurate selection, better still-**frame** facility and much longer life than tapes. Compare **optical disk**.

Video signal
The electrical signal that gives the picture on the **cathode ray tube** (CRT) in a television set or **monitor**. The television aerial signal has to be demodulated (see **modulation**) and separated from the sound so the picture quality is not as good as with a monitor, which accepts the video signal directly. Some computers, when used with a monitor, output separate red, green and blue video signals which drive the three electron guns in the tube.

Videotex
Any information service giving a display on the screen of a television set. The coded **data** may be transmitted as part of the broadcast television signal (**teletext**) or via the telephone system (**viewdata**). See also **Ceefax**, **Oracle**, **Prestel** and **Micronet 800**.

Viewdata

An information service in which data is sent over the telephone lines and displayed on a television set or computer terminal. The information comes from a large store held on a public or private computer, and subscribers can select the information they need. Viewdata is also an interactive, or two-way, service as it can be used for transmission of messages between, say, offices, homes, banks and shops, and for programmed learning, enquiries and so on.

Virtual memory

A way of artificially enlarging a computer's main **memory**, using a store management system that draws data or sections of a program from a fast-acting **backing store** when required. The computer changes the programmer's 'virtual' (imaginary) locations into actual locations as necessary.

Voice input/output

A method of inputting **instruction**s to a computer; or operating a mechanical or electrical device controlled by a **microprocessor**. Both depend upon **speech recognition**. Voice output is possible using 'speech synthesis', whereby the computer can be programmed to make noises similar to human speech.

Volatile memory

Memory that allows the **data** to disappear when the power is switched off. This happens with **core store**, **RAM chip**s and **silicon disk**s, but not with magnetic tape, disk, ROM chips or bubble memory.

Voltage regulator

A device that accepts electrical power with varying voltage levels and supplies power with an almost uniform voltage. Used with computers to prevent the corruption of data stored in memory.

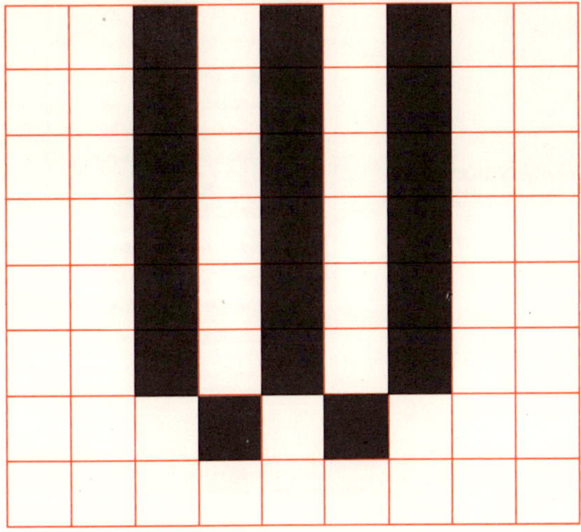

Wafer
A thin slice of silicon crystal or other **semiconductor** material, measuring about 10 centimetres (4 inches) in diameter, upon which several hundred **integrated circuits** (chips) can be built.

Waveform
A diagram showing the shape of an electrical wave that is being transmitted along a wire or cable or a sound wave through the air.

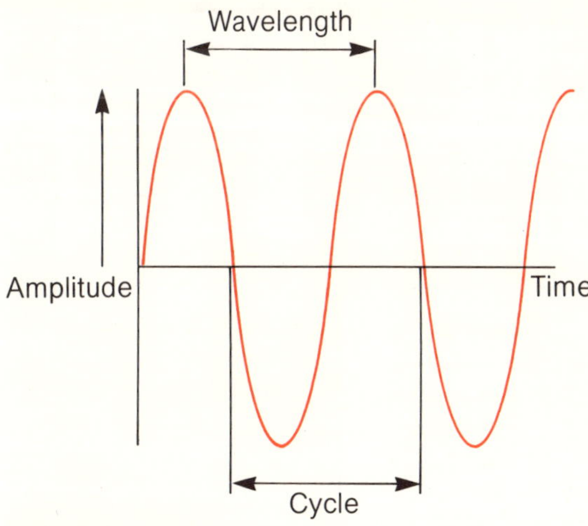

White noise
Electrical interference that produces an irregular buzzing or humming sound. It is caused by the electrical components in the **circuits** when they get warm. Noticeable with some microcomputers when they have been switched on for several hours.

Winchester disk drive
A sealed box that contains a fixed **hard disk** and **disk drive** unit. The **read/write head** is very close to the disk and this allows a smaller track width, and hence more recording tracks and much greater storage, than on a **floppy disk**.

Window
An area on a computer screen divided off from part of the display and showing something different. A small **text** window might describe the main picture, or a graphics window could show a chart beside the figures being listed.

Word
The number of **bits** that the computer stores and works with as a group at one time. It might be 8, 12, 16, 24, or 32. A bigger word size gives both larger **immediate access store** and faster operation. Most computers group data in small lengths, usually one **character**, and these are known as **bytes**. **Eight-bit** bytes are the most common.

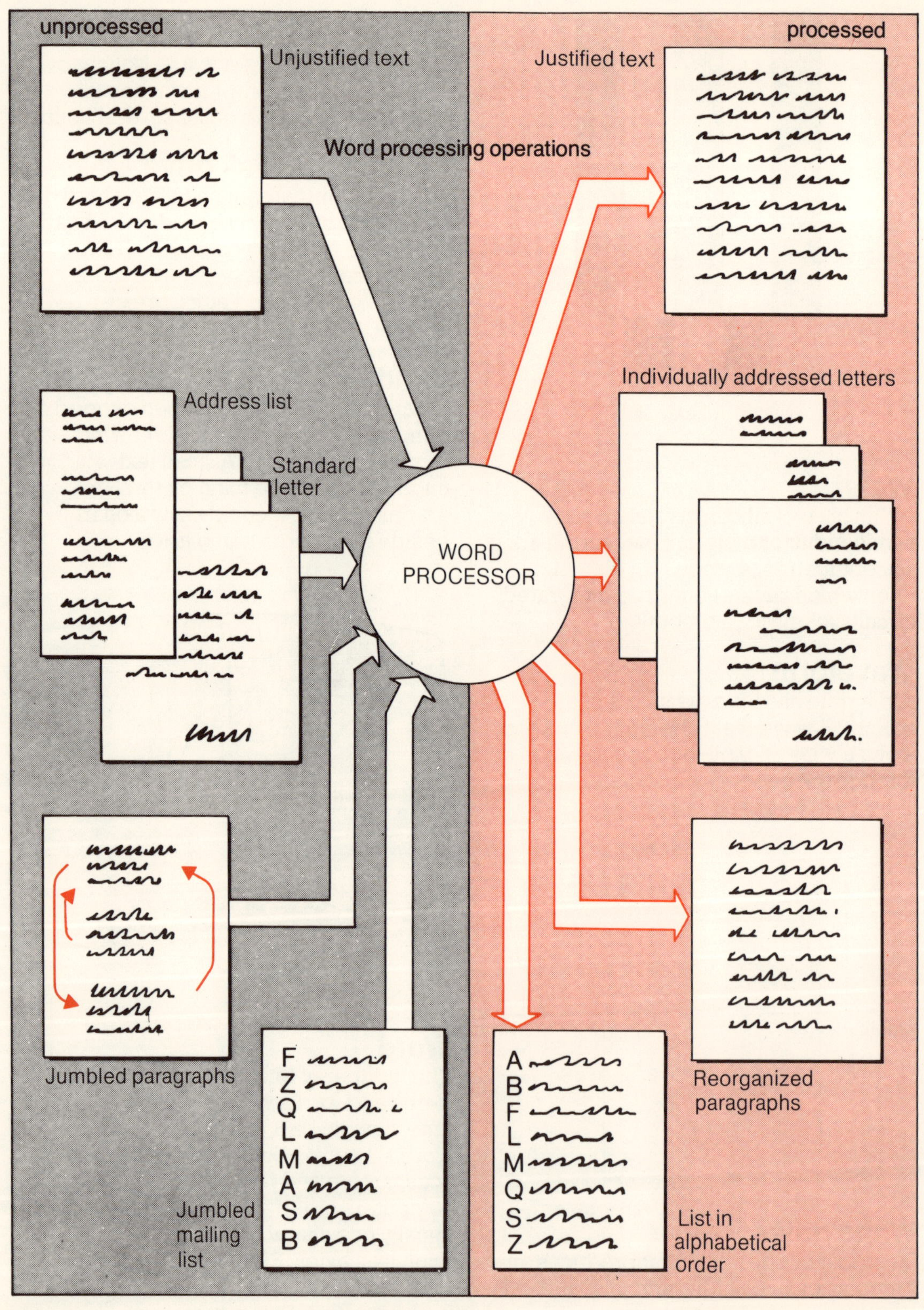
unprocessed
processed
Unjustified text
Justified text
Word processing operations
Address list
Standard letter
Individually addressed letters
WORD PROCESSOR
Jumbled paragraphs
Reorganized paragraphs
F
Z
Q
L
M
A
S
B
Jumbled mailing list
A
B
F
L
M
Q
S
Z
List in alphabetical order

Word processor

A computer system that allows the user to input, store, edit and print text. In addition it can control the layout, or **format**, of the printed output, **justify** the text, correct spelling, make deletions and add or move sentences or paragraphs. It can also add individual names or dates to standard letters from a mailing list **file**. Word processing **software** is available for most microcomputers but may not offer all the facilities of a 'dedicated' (purpose-built) processor.

Work station

A work desk or work area equipped with a **word processor** together with other computing facilities such as **information retrieval**, **electronic mail**, video phones and **database** access. The work station is tomorrow's desk with its modern communications.

Wrap

(1) When the computer screen display is full, taking the next line to the top of the screen and overwriting the line that was there before. The next new line will then appear below that one, and so on to the bottom of the screen. Compare **scroll**.
(2) When a line of text is broken at the right-hand edge of the screen, because it is too long for the screen's width, and is automatically carried over onto the next line. This can split a word into two.

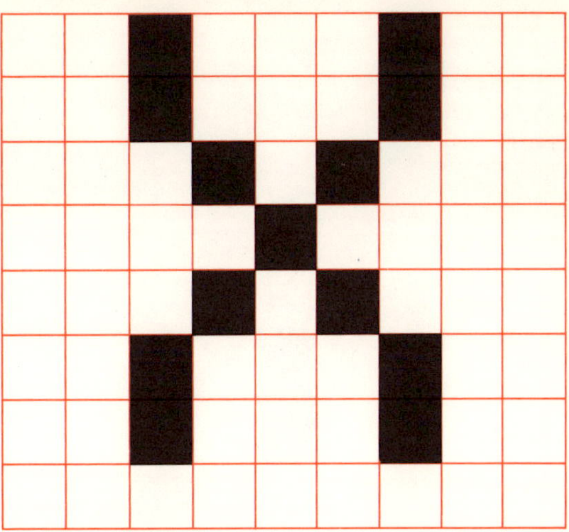

X co-ordinate

A number indicating the distance of a point from the left-hand side of a computer screen or piece of paper. On a graph, the number of columns across from the left-hand vertical (y-axis) line. Usually given with a Y co-ordinate to define the exact position of any point.

Xerographic printer

A printer that prints a page at a time using a process similar to that of a dry photocopier. The image is projected onto a charged plate and covered with a fine powder which adheres to its shape. This powder is then transferred to paper. Speeds of 50 pages per minute are possible.

X-Y Plotter

A **plotter** that draws according to the **X** and **Y co-ordinate**s that it is given. Used to display barcharts, line graphs, drawings and maps. Some can do shading while others have several pens for drawing in different colours. See **flat-bed plotter**.

Y co-ordinate

A number used to indicate the distance from the bottom of the screen or paper. On a graph, the number of rows up from the bottom (x-axis) line. With the X co-ordinate specifies a point.

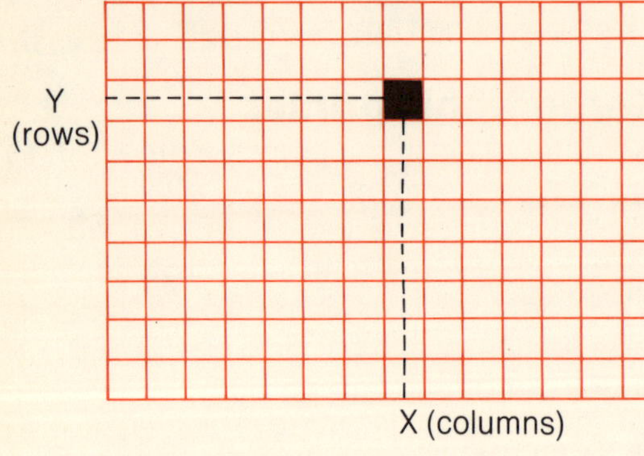

Zero-fill

The replacement of **data** in a **location** or locations by zeroes. A zero is written with a line through it, like this Ø, to distinguish it from the capital letter O.

Zone

(1) The top three positions on a **punched card**. To represent a non-numeric character, one of these positions has to be punched together with another hole in the same column.
(2) One of the vertical bands used by a microcomputer when printing on a screen. Usually there are four such zones with text being **left justified** and numbers **right justified** in each zone.